Vincent Ryan OSB

# Lent and Holy Week

Veritas Publications Dublin 1976

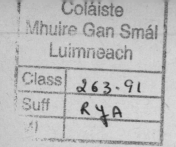
*First published 1976 by*
*Veritas Publications,*
*Pranstown House, Booterstown Avenue, Co. Dublin.*

*Typography by Liam Miller.*
*Cover by Steven Hope.*
*Set in 11 on 12 Baskerville.*
*Printed and bound in the Republic of Ireland by*
*Cahill and Co., Limited, Dublin.*

*Acknowledgment is made to the* International Committee
on English in the Liturgy *for quotations from the new*
Ro man Missal; the Talbot Press *for quotations from the*
*new Breviary, and Darton, Longman & Todd for*
*quotations from* The Jerusalem Bible.

*Nihil Obstat:*
*Richard Sherry, D.D.*
*Censor Deputatus.*

*Imprimi Potest:*
*Dom Augustine O'Sullivan, OSB*
*January 29, 1976.*

*IMPRIMATUR:*
*+Dermot,*
*Archbishop of Dublin*
*February 20, 1976.*

*The* nihil obstat *and* imprimatur *are a declaration that a*
*text is considered to be free of doctrinal or moral error.*
*They do not necessarily imply agreement with opinions*
*expressed by the author.*

*ISBN 0-905092-01-5*
*CAT. NO. 3330*

# Contents

|   | | Page |   |
|---|---|---|---|
|   | Introduction | *Page* | 7 |
| 1 | A programme for Lent | | 9 |
| 2 | Lent and penance | | 12 |
| 3 | Lent as preparation for baptism | | 27 |
| 4 | Lent and the passion of Christ | | 39 |
| 5 | Introducing Holy Week | | 48 |
| 6 | Passion or Palm Sunday | | 51 |
| 7 | Monday to Wednesday | | 56 |
| 8 | The Easter triduum | | 58 |
| 9 | Holy Thursday | | 62 |
| 10 | Good Friday | | 74 |
| 11 | Holy Saturday | | 80 |
| 12 | The Easter Vigil | | 91 |
| 13 | Easter Sunday | | 119 |
|   | Notes | | 128 |
|   | Bibliography | | 134 |

# Introduction

There is no lack of books on Lent and Holy Week. With very few exceptions, however, these have become dated as a result of the liturgical reforms of Vatican II. The value of even the best commentary is greatly diminished when it no longer corresponds to the current liturgical books. This small work is an attempt to fill the gap.

The reader will not find here a detailed commentary on the liturgy of Lent and Holy Week. My aim has been to present, as simply as possible, the essential message of this great period in the Church's year. The renewed liturgy offers us almost unlimited variety; and while this must be welcomed as an undoubted enrichment, it may also represent a source of confusion. We may simply fail "to see the wood for the trees". If this book succeeds in making a pathway through the wood, it will have achieved its purpose.

Even at the risk of some compression, it has seemed preferable to treat of Lent and Holy Week together. The reason for this is not merely one of convenience or economy; it lies rather in the fact that these two times form a unity, they are intrinsic parts of the paschal cycle.

From a study of the missal, lectionary and breviary, a vision of Lent and Easter emerges which is both noble and inspiring. It has been gratifying to discover how closely this vision or concept corresponds to that of tradition. We live in a world of change, and the liturgy must to some extent reflect the changing circumstances of our existence. But in the liturgy of the seasons there are deep and permanent values which the recent reforms have not only maintained but even revitalised.

I wish to acknowledge the valuable help given me by Fr Placid Murray, OSB in the writing and final drafting of this book. My sincere thanks to him, and also to Fr Oliver Crilly, Director of Veritas Publications, who encouraged me in the writing of it and waited patiently for its completion.

Vincent Ryan, OSB

# 1 A programme for Lent

Lent is not the rigorous time it used to be. For example, the fast has been greatly mitigated. During this "penitential season" life goes on much the same as at other times of the year. There is the ceremony of receiving ashes on our foreheads at the beginning of Lent and we may make a few good resolutions to undertake this or to do without that; but this does not really amount to very much in terms of generosity or self-sacrifice.

The Church has not gone soft on penance, however: she expects just as much of us now as in the past. The difference is that today we are treated more as adults than as children. The form that our Lenten penance will take is largely left to ourselves, it is not spelt out for us as in the past. The responsibility is entirely our own. It is a case of *noblesse oblige*.

Lent is no mere formality. It has not lost its relevance nor its challenge. It is still a demanding time, even if the Church does not lay down in detail what is required of us. It is not easy to respond to the call to conversion of heart, to penance and renewal made to us insistently during the weeks of Lent. The challenge to compare our lives with the word of God and to conform our lives with the Gospel is not lightly accepted. In the Lenten liturgy we are confronted day by day with the word of God judging us, challenging us and showing us up as we really are.

Lent is not easier now; if anything it is more difficult than it was in the past, provided we are prepared to enter into its spirit and to take it seriously. It must not be thought, however, that the effort is all our own. Looked at from God's point of view, it is a season of grace. It is God who takes the Church in hand, purifying it, renewing it and sanctifying it. This is aptly expressed in the second preface of Lent: "This great season of grace is *your gift to your family* to renew us in spirit."

In the Liturgy Constitution of Vatican II (art. 109) the Church describes the character of Lent and sets before us a programme for its observance:

> The season of Lent has a twofold character; primarily by recalling or preparing for baptism and penance, it disposes the faithful who persevere in hearing the word of God and in prayer, to celebrate the paschal mystery.

Baptism, penance, listening to the word of God, prayer and meditation on the passion of Christ are the principal elements which make up our Lenten programme.

In our observance of Lent let us not lose sight of our goal which is the worthy celebration of the paschal mystery. Lent and Easter are so closely joined as to form a unit. The grace of Easter is already operative during Lent strengthening and renewing the Church; the risen and glorified Lord

is at work among souls drawing them to himself;
Christ the Good Shepherd is searching for his lost
sheep during these weeks of preparation.

Lent is not an end in itself: it is directed towards
Easter and the joyful celebration of the pasch. St
Benedict, for example, in chapter 49 of his monastic
rule, urges his monks during the weeks of Lent to
look forward "to the holy feast of Easter with the
joy of spiritual desire". We find this idea of expectation and preparation expressed again and again in
the liturgy, as, for example, in the opening prayer
for Friday of the second week in Lent:

> Merciful Father,
> may our acts of penance
>    bring us your forgiveness,
> open our hearts to your love,
> and prepare us for the coming feast of the
>    resurrection.

Let us now explore the three great Lenten
themes: penance, baptism and the passion of Christ,
in the light of the revised missal, lectionary and
breviary of the post-Vatican Church.

# 2   Lent and penance

## Penance as conversion

The reception of ashes at the beginning of Lent recalls the time when public penitents wore sackcloth and ashes as a sign of their repentance. Since about the tenth century it has been the custom for all the faithful to receive ashes on their foreheads on this first day of Lent. This ceremony manifests the Church's willingness to undergo penance. It is as though all of us, from the Pope down, were included among the ranks of the public penitents.

It is important that we have a clear idea of what penance means. Too easily we equate it with some of its external expressions, for example, fasting and abstinence. These are indeed manifestations of penance but they do not constitute the full reality. The Christian notion of penance goes much deeper than that. Let us try to understand it in the light of sacred Scripture and the Church's teaching.

Penance is one of the constant themes of both Old and New Testaments. The Greek word for penance, *metanoia*, conveys the idea of conversion or change of heart. This implies that penance involves an inner change in man, a turning to God, a re-orientation of our lives towards God. It also implies

12

a turning away from sin, a rejection of all that was evil in our lives. Penance affects us at the very roots of our being.

This change of heart or conversion presupposes a *call* from God. It is he who calls us and gives us the grace to respond. During the season of Lent the Church will often pray for the grace of conversion, as, for example, in this prayer for Monday of the first week:

> *Turn our hearts back to you,* God our saviour;
> form us by your heavenly teaching,
> so that we may truly profit by our Lenten
>   observance.

This conversion need not be sudden or dramatic, as it was with St Paul or St Augustine. It may be gradual and imperceptible, an ongoing activity in our lives. The call to conversion is always there and so our response must be continuous.

The presence of sin in our lives makes penance or conversion necessary at all times. If we feel that we have nothing whatever to reproach ourselves with, we should listen to the blunt words of St John:

> If we say we have no sin in us, we are deceiving
> ourselves and refusing to admit the truth
> *(1 Jn 1:8)..*

Penance, in the sense of conversion, is never optional. Even when we have long since resolved to give our lives for God, our conversion is never complete and total. There remain corners of our heart never fully converted to the Gospel, pockets of resistance to God's grace; we have always to contend with our limitations and failures. Only God can create a new heart within us.

In the lives of those who have estranged themselves from God through grave sin, conversion is all the more urgent. When God in his mercy bestows on them the grace of conversion they must not delay in responding to his grace. Moral inertia and cowardice will suggest a thousand reasons for delay; one recalls the plea of the young Augustine: "Lord, grant me continence, *but not yet*."

There are times when the voice of God calling us to repentance is more pressing and insistent than at others. The season of Lent is a time when the whole Church is called to penance and conversion. It is a God-given opportunity to undertake the conversion of our hearts. In the words of Scripture, quoted in the liturgy of Ash Wednesday:

> At the favourable time, I have listened to you; on the day of salvation I came to your help. Well, now is the favourable time; this is the day of salvation *(2 Cor 6:2)*.

And in the words of the psalmist which we hear at the beginning of the daily office: "O that today you would listen to his voice!"

## The practice of penance

While the essence of penance consists in a sincere change of heart, it also requires visible expression in our life and conduct. This leads us to speak of the "observance of Lent" and the traditional penitential exercises which are associated with this season.

We may sum up the whole Lenten observance in a single word, and this is the word "service": a more perfect service of God and of neighbour; service of God in prayer, worship, self-denial and a more active faith; service of our fellow human-beings in a greater readiness to respond to their needs.

To put it in another way, our Lenten observance consists in giving and forgiving. We must give not only external things such as money and possessions, but also such precious things as our time and sympathy, making ourselves available to other people even when that may cause us serious inconvenience.

We must also forgive. The practice of mutual pardon is all-important and we are reminded of it again and again in the liturgy. Two important gospel texts confront us with this message during the first week of Lent. The first, read on Tuesday, recounts our Lord's teaching of the "Our Father" to his disciples (Mt 6:7-15). This passage contains not only the formula of the Lord's Prayer but also the very important addition on the necessity of mutual pardon:

> Yes, if you forgive others their failings, your heavenly Father will forgive you yours; but if you do not forgive others, your Father will not forgive your failings either.

Then on Friday of the first week the gospel (Mt 5: 20-26) instructs us on the need to be reconciled with our offended brother before we bring our offering to the altar.

In one of his Lenten sermons Pope St Leo added

his own reflections to this gospel message. Easter, he said, is the feast of divine pardon; it celebrates man's reconciliation with God through the sacrifice of Christ. It is appropriate that we prepare for it by pardoning one another and being reconciled with those estranged from us.[1]

## Fasting, almsgiving and prayer

Among the traditional works of penance special importance has always been attached to fasting, almsgiving and prayer. Already in the Old Testament these practices were highly valued. They are so closely related as to form a kind of unity.

Fasting during Lent, however, has been greatly modified. We are now obliged to fast on two days only: Ash Wednesday and Good Friday.[2] We are encouraged to fast throughout the whole of Lent, but this is a counsel and not a commandment. For some this is a sign that the Church has abandoned penance and that practices such as fasting have been set aside.

The Church has not done so, but in mitigating the fast she is motivated by pastoral considerations. Not all are equal to the rigours of a prolonged fast. Health, age and the kind of work in which people are engaged have to be considered. The Church today therefore requires of all the faithful only a bare minimum of fasting.

But the example of Christ himself, the constant tradition of the Church and the abiding need for penance do not permit us simply to ignore fasting. It continues as an important element of Christian asceticism, an ideal not only to be valued but also realised to some degree by all of us.

Let us consider for a moment the purpose of the fast. It would be a mistake to consider it merely in a negative sense. The fast is not an end in itself. It is good to practise moderation and restraint, but these are not specifically Christian virtues. The fast must have a higher purpose: its ultimate object is not the subjugation of the body and its appetites but, rather, more perfect love of God and neighbour.

The prophets and Christ himself have warned against the dangers of mere formalism. Where love is absent no amount of fasting will please God. This is trenchantly expressed in the words of Isaiah, read at Mass on the Friday after Ash Wednesday:

> Is not this the sort of fast that pleases me—it is the Lord who speaks— to break unjust fetters and undo the thongs of the yoke, to let the oppressed go free, and break every yoke, to share your bread with the hungry and shelter the homeless poor *(Is 58:6-7)*.

Fasting, if it is to measure up to the ideal expressed in the prophets and the gospels, must be completed by generous acts of practical charity.

There is a close connection between fasting and almsgiving. This is an idea which has been rediscovered in recent years, and one which gives a whole new motivation to our fast. What is saved by restricting ourselves in food, luxuries, entertainment, etc. is given away as alms to the poor. This is known as "the fast of sharing", and is widely practised by families and religious communities today.

This idea was often expressed in the writings of the fathers, for example Pope St Leo and Pope St Gregory the Great. It is also witnessed to in the texts of the Lenten liturgy. Let us take a few examples. The office of readings during Lent has two fine sermons relating fasting with almsgiving. The first, read on Monday of the first week, is by St Gregory Nazianzen. In it he exhorts us, as good stewards of God's gifts, to show kindness and love to all people, but especially to the poor. Then on Tuesday of the third week we have that beautiful sermon of St Peter Chrysologus, which begins:

> There are three things, brethren, three, through which faith stands firm, devotion abides, and virtue endures; prayer, fasting and mercy. What prayer knocks for upon a door, fasting successfully begs and mercy receives. Prayer, fasting and mercy: these three are a unit. They give life to one another. For, fasting is the soul of prayer; and mercy is the life of fasting.

There are so many worthy causes to which we can contribute: the St Vincent de Paul Society, for example, and organisations for assistance to under-developed nations and for the relief of famine, such as Trócaire. What we save from our self-imposed fasts, from our restrictions in such things as alcohol, tobacco, entertainment, etc., we should put to generous use. This requires a very real spirit of sacrifice.

St Raymund of Penafort had a great love for the poor. He liked to call them his creditors. It is in this spirit that we should assist the poor. Our Lenten

fast should not be merely an exercise in thrift. Like
St Raymund, we should regard the money we have
saved as belonging by right to the poor. We are
their debtors.

Lent has also been likened to a retreat or mission;
not just a parish or community retreat, but a retreat
for the whole Church. In a retreat we set aside as
much time as possible for prayer. Likewise, in this
Lenten retreat the Church's prayer is more intense
and continuous.

There is a close kinship between prayer and
fasting. In the gospel for the first Sunday of Lent
*(Mt 4:1-11)*, which describes the temptation of
Jesus, our Lord rebukes Satan who challenged him
to change the stones into loaves of bread: "Man
does not live on bread alone but on every word
that comes from the mouth of God." The word of
God is also food, it is the bread of life. It is *cibus
cibo melior*, food more substantial than food itself,
to quote an inscription found on a monastic
lectern. To the extent that we abstain from material
food, our souls should hunger more and more for
this spiritual food.

In the celebration of Mass, the faithful are
nourished both at the table of God's word and at
the table of his sacrament; word and eucharist are
complementary forms of sustenance. The Mass is
our sacrifice, our nourishment and our greatest
prayer. And so among the traditional practices of
Lent, that of daily attendance at Mass and communion deserves the highest recommendation.[3]

Listening to the word of God is an essential part
of prayer. It is very important to be open and

receptive to the word of God. It is a word which is alive and efficacious. How well this is expressed in the text from Isaiah which is read at Mass on Tuesday of the first week:

> Yes, as the rain and the snow come down from the heavens and do not return without watering the earth, making it yield and giving growth to provide seed for the sower and bread for the eating, so the word that goes from my mouth does not return to me empty, without carrying out my will and succeeding in what it was sent to do *(Is 55:10-11)*.

During the six weeks of Lent the Liturgy of the Word, both in the eucharist and the prayer of the hours, is especially abundant and varied. We have but to listen to it, reflect on it in our hearts and allow it to act upon us.

Prayer is a dialogue in which listening is as important as speaking. As partners in the dialogue, we must be sensitive and receptive to the voice of God. This has been described as the art of conversing with Jesus, the imitation of Christ, and there is a prayer in the new Roman missal which expresses this concisely and with feeling. It is from the second Sunday of Lent and is obviously inspired by the gospel of the day which tells of the transfiguration of Christ:

> God our Father
> you bid us listen to your Son, the well-beloved.
> Nourish our hearts on your word,
> purify the eyes of our mind *(Breviary* version).

What Christ asks of us in prayer may be difficult: we may be required to renounce this or to undertake that. The word of God is indeed a "two-edged sword"; that is why we may be rather afraid of prayer. The fact that it is demanding makes it an effective part of our penance. True conversion of heart presupposes a willingness on our part to hear and to heed what God asks of us. Our attitude should be: "Speak, Lord, for your servant is listening."

In the dialogue which is prayer, we can also address the Father through and in his Son or speak directly to Christ. Prayer, founded on faith in Christ, is always efficacious. Tertullian expresses this belief in a bold phrase found in the office of readings for Thursday of the third week of Lent: "Prayer alone it is that conquers God." In the gospel for Thursday of the first week, we have Christ's own promise: "Ask, and it will be given to you; search, and you will find; knock, and the door will be opened to you" *(Mt 7:7)*.

In a season of penance it is natural that we should pray for pardon, pardon for our own sins and for those of others. We make our own the humble admission of guilt which Daniel uttered on behalf of his people: "We have sinned, we have done wrong, we have acted wickedly, we have betrayed your commandments and your ordinances" *(Dn 9: 4-10,* read at Mass on Monday of the second week). The great prayer of Moses pleading for his rebellious people is also a fitting expression of the Church's prayer: "Lord, why should your wrath blaze against this people of yours whom you brought out of the

land of Egypt?.... Leave your burning wrath; relent
and do not bring this disaster on your people"
(*Ex 32:7-14*, read at Mass on Thursday of the
fourth week).

### A Lenten trilogy

Prayer which is joined to fasting and almsgiving
is good, for almsgiving will purge away every
sin. . . (*Tob 12:8-9*, the responsory for Wednesday of the third week).

Fasting supplies us with the means to practice
almsgiving. It is also conducive to prayer. It
increases our hunger for God's word and sacrament,
and for God himself. Note how the prayers of the
Mass express this thought: "Through the discipline
of Lent help us to grow in our desire for you"
(Opening prayer, Tuesday of first week); "May we
who receive this sacrament restrain our earthly
desires and grow in love for the things of heaven"
(Prayer after communion, same day).

On the third Sunday of Lent we have the following short prayer which sums up all that we have
been saying on the subject of fasting, almsgiving
and prayer:

Father, you have taught us to overcome our
sins by prayer, fasting and works of mercy.
When we are discouraged by our weakness, give
us confidence in your love.

### The sacrament of penance

The 1974 Order of Penance strongly recommends

the practice of sacramental confession at this season.[4] In article 13 it states:

> The season of Lent is especially suitable for the celebration of the sacrament of|penance, for on Ash Wednesday the faithful are admonished: "Repent and believe the Gospel." It is appropriate, therefore, to arrange for frequent penitential services during Lent, so that all the faithful might be offered the opportunity of being reconciled to God and their brothers and of celebrating the paschal mystery with renewed heart during the holy triduum.

The sacrament of penance has been instituted expressly for the forgiveness of sins. Through the ministry of the priest, who acts in the name of Christ and through his power, God's pardon is bestowed on the penitent who confesses his sins and is rightly disposed.

It is regrettable that in recent years this sacrament has been neglected. If only people realised that it is a sign and an instrument of God's love, they would not neglect it as they do. Humanly speaking, it may be distasteful but, viewed in the light of faith, it is a sure means of advancing along the road of conversion, of breaking free from the attachment to sin and of growing in the love of God.

Great thought and care have gone into the preparation of the new Order of Penance. Its adoption and implementation throughout the whole Catholic Church may well mark the renewal of the sacrament of penance. In fact, signs of such a renewal are already in evidence.[5]

The rite of penance may now take two forms: private or individual penance and public or communal penance. Individual penance will always continue alongside the more communal forms of penance. What is known as "confession of devotion" is still encouraged. The new Order says in article 7: "For the one who falls consistently into venial sin through weakness, a frequent recourse to the sacrament of penance will bring strength, and will lead him to the fullness of freedom of the sons of God."

At least once during Lent we should avail of this individual form of penance. Our aim should be to make it something of an occasion. A routine, hurried performance is unsatisfactory for both priest and penitent. It should be calm, unhurried and prayerful. It should not be a monologue or catalogue of sins, but a dialogue between priest and penitent.

Prepare your confession well and choose a time when your confessor is not too busy. Think of the sacrament as a meeting between you and Christ. Look on the priest as Christ's representative. Make it easy for him to exercise his pastoral role: he is there not just as a judge but as a friend and counsellor. When necessary, he is only too glad to help you formulate your confession and where there is a real exchange between the two partners, the sacrament will be very fruitful: an atmosphere of mutual trust is built up and the priest is in a position to shed the light of the Gospel on our lives.

For most of us, communal penance is something new. For historians of the liturgy it is not really so new, for it has much in common with the discipline of public penance as it was known and practised in the early centuries of the Church. The new rites of communal penance, however, have none of the harshness of the public penance of antiquity.

All that was good and positive in the ancient discipline of public penance has been restored. The 1974 Order provides two forms of communal celebration of penance. In the first, the celebration of the word of God is followed by individual confession and absolution. In the second form, which is more restricted in use, individual confession of sins is omitted and the priest gives a general absolution. Provision is also made for a non-sacramental service of penance.

In justification of communal penance the Order declares in article 22: "A common celebration manifests more clearly the ecclesial nature of penance." In other words it is the whole Church, the *ecclesia*, and especially the local church, the local community, which is involved. Our sins are not only an offence against God but also against his Church and since the Church is the body of Christ, it follows that the lives of its members interact. The good we do redounds to the good of the whole organism; our sins and failures impair the life of the Church.

One of the aims of communal penance is to impress on us an awareness of the social dimension and consequences of sin. We are accountable not only for our own personal sins but also, to some extent, for the sins of the society to which we belong. If there are injuries in our society, such as discrimination against minority groups or gross neglect of the weaker members of the community— the poor, old-age pensioners, etc. — then we must all examine our consciences.

It is especially appropriate that communal celebrations of penance take place during Lent; for, as we have seen, during this season it is the whole Church which undertakes penance. We have all sinned and all of us seek to be reconciled with God. In this great work of reconciliation we can help one another by prayer and example. The new Order expressly says this in article 8: "The whole Church, as a priestly people, has a part to play in the work of reconciliation entrusted to it." Our reconciliation with God will come about through the Church and through the sacraments. Our penance implies reconciliation with the Church and with our fellow-men whom we have injured by our sins. It is in a communal celebration of penance that all these social and ecclesial aspects of penance come to the fore.

# 3  Lent as preparation for baptism

## Joining the catechumens

We have likened Lent to a retreat or mission for the whole Church. One of the climaxes of a parish retreat is the renewal of baptismal promises by the whole congregation. One of the great climactic moments of the Easter liturgy is the same solemn ceremony of renewal in the course of the paschal vigil; during the weeks of Lent the Church is preparing us for that moment.

Traditionally, Easter is the most appropriate time for the conferring of baptism; the weeks of Lent represent the time of immediate preparation for this event. In the fifth and sixth centuries adult baptism was still the norm in Rome, and in the weeks immediately preceding Easter, the catechumens underwent a fairly intense preparation. This consisted of frequent meetings for prayers and instruction, blessings and exorcisms, as well as the learning of certain prayers.

It is good for us to recall what a difficult and even hazardous undertaking baptism was in the early centuries. It was a serious commitment exposing the candidate to the mistrust, ridicule or open persecution of the pagan society around him. It was not lightly undertaken, and the Church hesitated to confer baptism on those who gave little evidence of being serious in their intentions.

To be baptised meant, both literally and meta-phorically, to take the plunge; literally, because baptism was by immersion; metaphorically, because it implied a once-for-all commitment and the adoption of a whole new way of life.

For the majority of Christians, baptised in infancy, no such commitment was involved. It is vitally important, however, that we do not remain Christians in name only but that each one of us ratifies his or her baptism at an age when this becomes possible. One such occasion is confirma-tion when the child renews the promises made on his behalf at baptism. There will be many other oc-casions throughout adult life; baptism is, after all, a permanent sacrament.

During Lent we prepare to renew our baptismal obligations at Easter. The Church invites us to join the ranks of the adult catechumens. In their com-pany we can learn what it means to be a Christian. We follow them in their pilgrimage of faith.

The ancient liturgy of the catechumenate has in our own times been revived. This is one of the most interesting features of the new rites of adult bap-tism.[1] It shows that the Church recognises the need for preparatory stages leading up to baptism; each of these stages is sanctified by appropriate rites. It all takes place within the liturgical frame-work of Lent and Holy Week.

On the first Sunday of Lent the catechumens are formally inscribed for baptism. This takes place in a little ceremony included within the Mass rite. The Church has now accepted them as candidates for the sacraments of Christian initiation. On the third, fourth and fifth Sundays of Lent, these candidates (*electi*, chosen ones, to use the ancient title) are again assembled in church to hear the word of God and receive the Church's blessing. As we shall see, the whole liturgy of the word for these Sundays is aimed at their instruction.

Also during Lent the ceremony of the "traditions" takes place. That is the solemn "tradition" or handing over to the catechumens of the two most precious formulas in Christian faith and piety: the Apostles' Creed and the Lord's Prayer. They are entrusted with these prayers which they are to learn and treasure.

During Lent we offer special prayers for the catechumens because the Church knows that they need prayer if they are to persevere. They may be troubled by temptations against faith or daunted by the demands the Christian life will make on them. The prayer and encouragement of the baptised members of the Church will be their great support in these weeks leading up to their baptism.

## The baptismal readings

We have referred to the third, fourth and fifth Sundays of Lent as being of special significance for the catechumens. The readings were chosen to throw light on the mystery of baptism. In the new Roman lectionary these traditional readings have been restored to the Sunday liturgy. Strictly speaking, they belong to the first year of the three-year cycle but for pastoral reasons may be used in the other years as well.

The gospel texts are of special importance. They are all from St John: *Jn 4:5-42* (The water of life); *Jn 9:1-41* (Baptism as enlightenment); *Jn 11:1-45* (Baptism as resurrection). They are instructive not only for the catechumens but for us, the baptised, as well. In a real sense we are all learners, mere apprentices in the Christian life. The Church makes use of the liturgy to teach us about the mysteries of our faith. Baptism, by which we are inserted into the body of Christ, is a sacrament which we may never take for granted.

Of particular interest on these Sundays of Lent is the unified theme presented by the liturgy. The Church has arranged that the readings and other texts proper to these Sundays all in some way converge on the message of the gospel. The theme may be announced in the entrance antiphon or opening prayer, foreshadowed in the Old Testament reading, taken up again in the preface and echoed in the communion antiphon.

Let us now take a look at these Sunday readings with the intention of drawing from them all that they have to teach us about the sacrament of baptism and our life in Christ which follows from it.

## The water of life

On this third Sunday of Lent the three readings of the Mass allude to water, the symbol of baptism. In the passage from Exodus *(17:3-7)* we recall how

Moses struck the rock in the desert. He struck it with his staff and water flowed from it for all the people to drink.

In the second reading *(Rm 5:1-2, 5-8)* St Paul uses the analogy of water to describe the action of the Holy Spirit in our lives: "The love of God has been poured into our hearts by the Holy Spirit which has been given us."

The gospel *(Jn 4:5-42)* recounts our Lord's discourse with the Samaritan woman at the well of Sychar. He tells her about a mysterious gift of water which he has to offer: it is God's gift, whoever drinks it will never thirst again; it will become a spring inside one, welling up to eternal life.

The fathers of the Church have explained this gospel in the context of Christian baptism. It lends itself very well to a baptismal interpretation, and that is how the catechumens of old would have understood it. This we ourselves may legitimately do, without, however, interpreting it too narrowly in this sense. For the "gift of God" and the "living water" represent not just a sacrament but Christ himself. "Living water" in the Old Testament symbolises wisdom and truth, the riches contained in revelation. Here it refers to the life-giving teaching of Christ, who is incarnate wisdom. It is Christ's revelation of himself and must be assimilated. Here the action of the Holy Spirit comes into play: only then will it become a "spring inside him, welling up to eternal life".[2]

In this gospel Christ shows himself to be an excellent teacher. He is patient with the woman whom he meets at the well. He begins by arousing her curiosity and then leads her step by step to the knowledge that he is the Christ. The request for a drink of water was but a pretext to disclose to her the gift of God. It was really the woman's faith that he sought according to St Augustine, whose homily on this gospel we should read in the office of readings for this Sunday (*Divine Office*, II, pp. 146-48).

Notice how the preface echoes this thought of St Augustine and develops it:

> When he asked the woman of Samaria
>     for water to drink,
> Christ had already prepared for her
>     the gift of faith.
> In his thirst to receive her faith
> he awakened in her heart the fire of your love.

Faith and baptism are closely related. Baptism is a sacrament of faith. If we are already baptised let us give thanks for the gift of God and pray for an ever deepening faith.

## Baptism as enlightenment

On the fourth Sunday of Lent the theme of light prevails. When one considers that one of the terms for baptism in the early Church was enlightenment (*photismos*), it is clear that the readings, especially the gospel, have been very aptly chosen.

The ritual of baptism includes an anointing as well as a washing or immersion in water. This is reflected in the first reading from the first book of Samuel *(16:1, 6-7, 10-13)* which describes the anointing of David as king of Israel. This harmonises

with the gospel text in which there is also an anointing: Jesus anoints the eyes of the blind man with
clay and spittle and sends him to wash in the Pool
of Siloam where his sight is restored.

Between these two readings we have a text from
St Paul *(Eph 5:8-14)* in which light is not only a
symbol of baptism but of the whole Christian life.
At the end of this reading we have what appears to
be a fragment of an early baptismal hymn: "Wake
up from your sleep, rise from the dead, and Christ
will shine on you." But it is the gospel *(Jn 9:1-41)*
which commands our attention. Here Jesus makes
his great claim that he is "the light of the world".

The Church fathers saw in the pool of Siloam a
symbol of the baptismal font in which men, blinded
by ignorance and sin, have their sight restored and
begin to know God as he really is. Here is how St
Augustine comments on this text in one of his
homilies:[3]

> The blind man represents the human race. This
> blindness was, in the first man, the result of
> original sin, and it has communicated to us all,
> not only the seed of death, but also that of ini-
> quity... He (the blind man) washed in the pool
> which is interpreted "sent"; he was baptised in
> Christ... Let them (the catechumens) then has-
> ten unto this pool of salvation, if they seek the
> light.

Faith and baptism are so closely associated that
the symbol of light relates to both. The convert is
one who "sees the light", that is, he is drawn by
the gift of faith to the knowledge of God. In the

sacrament of baptism he is further "enlightened",
receiving the light of grace. This light, which is
given to us here below through faith and baptism,
will be perfected in heaven in that vision of God
which is called the "light of glory". St Augustine
contemplates this aspect of the gospel in his homily
given in the breviary for this Sunday (*Divine Office*
II, pp. 173-74).

## Baptism as resurrection

On the fifth Sunday of Lent, the theme is resurrection and new life. In the first reading *(Ez 37:12-14)*
the prophet Ezekiel foretells the return of his
people from exile under the image of a resurrection.
In the second reading *(Rm 8:8-11)*, St Paul speaks
explicitly of the resurrection of our bodies through
"the Spirit of him who raised Jesus from the dead".

The gospel *(Jn 11:1-45)* recounts the miracle of
the raising of Lazarus. It is a gospel we are very
familiar with since it occurs so often at funeral
Masses. On the occasion of a personal bereavement
we draw comfort from those great words:"I am the
resurrection. If anyone believes in me, even though
he dies he will live, and whoever lives and believes
in me will never die."

In this gospel we see Jesus at his most human
(weeping at the grave of Lazarus) and at his most
divine (working his greatest miracle in raising
Lazarus). This thought is also evoked in the preface:

As a man like us, Jesus wept for Lazarus
    his friend.

> As the eternal God, he raised Lazarus
> from the dead.

The next line of the preface connects the gospel with the new life conferred through baptism:

> Christ gave us the sacraments to lift us up
> to everlasting life.

We will now briefly explore this connection between the raising of Lazarus and the mystery of baptism.[4]

The raising of Lazarus is a *sign* of the resurrection of Jesus. It is a miracle which reveals his power over life and death; it authenticates his claim to be the resurrection and the life. It is also a sign of our own future resurrection through our union with Christ.

It is faith which establishes that union with Christ who is the source of our resurrection. Jesus leads Martha to an ever deeper faith in himself and each question elicits from her a more explicit act of faith. That is the response required of all of us if we are to enter fully into the life which Christ brings.

Baptism puts the seal to our faith. Through faith and baptism we already share in the life of the risen Christ. This is the great mystery which we will celebrate at Easter, in the light of the resurrection itself. That mystery is symbolised and foreshadowed in the raising of Lazarus.

## The sacrament of faith

When one compares the three readings from the gospel of St John, which we have discussed above, a similar pattern emerges: an encounter, a discourse, a sign and a profession of faith.

In each incident Jesus makes a great claim. To the Samaritan woman he offers "living water" and declares that he is the Messiah; to the man healed of his blindness he reveals that he is "the light of the world". To Martha he makes the greatest claim of all: "I am the resurrection."

It is revealing to compare the different responses Jesus meets with. The Samaritan woman by her very questioning expresses the beginning of faith: "I wonder if he is the Christ." The man healed of blindness makes a silent profession of faith: he falls down and worships Christ. Martha goes even further in her response of faith: "Yes, Lord, I believe that you are the Christ, the Son of God, the one who was to come into the world."

Christ offers us light, truth and eternal life; he offers us a share in his own divine life. In return he looks for the response of faith. That response is all-important. It is especially important in those preparing for baptism, but Lent is a time for all of us to awaken and deepen our faith.

## Reminders of baptism

Certain devotional practices and familiar prayers have an association with baptism, and so may be employed as reminders of our baptism.

When we make the sign of the cross we recall the day of our baptism when we received this sign "on our foreheads and in our hearts". It is as though Christ took possession of us by this sign. In tracing it on the child's forehead, the priest says: "In its name I claim you for Christ our Saviour by the sign of his cross." To make this sign slowly and reverently would be one good way of recalling our baptism during Lent.

The use of holy water is a very obvious reminder of baptism. To use it as a conscious reminder of this sacrament is an effective way of renewing the grace of our baptism. The Church has now introduced the blessing of holy water into the ritual of the Mass. It may replace the penitential rite. The water is blessed, the sacrament of baptism is recalled and the people are sprinkled. It would be very fitting if on the Sundays of Lent, especially the third, fourth and fifth when the Liturgy of the Word makes special reference to baptism, that this simple rite of blessing and sprinkling would be used as a collective recalling of baptism.

The Apostles' Creed and the "Our Father" are two important prayers closely associated with baptism. The former is a baptismal profession of faith. It expresses in summary form all the articles of Christian faith. It reminds us that we have received the sacrament of faith and that we are called upon to make our lives a living expression of that faith. The Lord's Prayer, or "Our Father", is the prayer *par excellence* of the baptised; it is the prayer of those who have received the "spirit of adoption" and may address God as Father. Christians of antiquity made a point of reciting it thrice daily. St Cyprian said this about it:

> What deep mysteries, my dearest brothers, are contained in the Lord's prayer! How many and

great they are! They are expressed in a few
words but they are rich in spiritual power so
that nothing is left out; every petition and
prayer we have to make is included. It is a com-
pendium of heavenly doctrine (*Divine Office*
III, p. 194; Office of readings for Monday,
week 11 of year).

# 4    Lent and the passion of Christ

The theme of Christ's passion is never absent from
the Lenten liturgy; it is there from the beginning,
but gathers momentum as the weeks progress. We
meet it in a hidden manner in the gospel of the
first Sunday *(Mt 4:1-11)* which describes the temptation of Jesus. There we see the Lord in his first
open confrontation with Satan. The scene is set for
the final struggle from which Christ will emerge
victorious. He rejects all the allurements of the
Prince of Darkness and chooses the way of obedience which will lead him to his passion and cross.

We meet the passion of Christ in an unexpected
manner in the scene of the transfiguration, which
provides the gospel reading for the second Sunday
of Lent *(Mt 17:1-9; Mk 9:2-10; Lk 9:28-36)*. The
mystery of Christ's transfiguration was intended to
strengthen the faith of the three chosen apostles,
Peter, John and James; it was to prepare them for
the passion and the "scandal of the cross". It is
Luke who tells us that Moses and Elijah spoke to
Christ "of his passing which he was to accomplish
in Jerusalem". The preface of the second Sunday
expands on this particular thought:

> On your holy mountain he revealed himself
> in glory

39

in the presence of his disciples.
He had already prepared them
    for his approaching death.
He wanted to teach them
    through the Law and the Prophets
that the promised Christ had first to suffer
and so come to the glory of his resurrection.

In the readings for Friday of the second week we find a mysterious but express allusion to the death of Christ. In the Old Testament reading *(Gen 37:3-4, 12-13, 17-28)*, it is foreshadowed in the plot to kill Joseph. In the gospel *(Mt 21:33-43, 45-46)*, Jesus foretells his own violent death in the parable of the vineyard and the wicked tenants who killed the son of the landowner.

## Ascent to the cross

Jesus freely advances towards his sacrifice. Each evangelist underlines the voluntary character of his sufferings and sacrificial death. The idea of an ascent to the cross is suggested by St Matthew in his gospel read on Wednesday of the second week:

Now we are going up to Jerusalem, and the Son of Man is about to be handed over to the chief priests and scribes. They will condemn him to death and will hand him over to the pagans to be mocked and scourged and crucified; and on the third day he will rise again *(Mt 20:17-28)*.

The final journey is an ascent to Jerusalem, to Calvary and, beyond the cross, to glory. It is an ascent and an ascension. St Luke expresses this with special clarity in his gospel *(Lk 9:51)*: "Now as the time drew near for him to be taken up to heaven, he resolutely took the road for Jerusalem and sent messengers ahead of him."

There is a great finality about that decision. Christ makes it in the clear foreknowledge of what lies ahead for him. The disciples are filled with forebodings, but for their master there can be no turning back: for this he came into the world.

## Mounting opposition

During the fourth and fifth weeks of Lent the Church sets before us each day the gospel of St John. In the selected passages from chapters five to twelve we follow Christ, stage by stage, through the events leading up to his arrest and condemnation. St John conveys extremely well the atmosphere of tension and conflict. Christ is presented to us in daily confrontation with the Pharisees.

There is no dissimulation on Christ's part; he reveals who he is. He makes the great claim that he is one with the Father, that he is the Son of God. And it is this unequivocal assertion which arouses the fury of his accusers: "But that only made the Jews even more intent on killing him, because not content with breaking the sabbath, he spoke of God as his own Father, and so made himself God's equal" (*Jn 5:18*; see also the gospel for Wednesday of fourth week).

The words of Christ evoke a response: fury on the part of his enemies, faith on the part of those who are prepared to listen and to take his words to heart. They are a challenge to us too. Christ addresses us in the gospels, eliciting from us the response of faith. The gospels are not a record of the past but a living message to us men and women of today.

On Friday of the fourth week, the plot to kill Jesus is foretold in the first reading *(Wis 2:1, 12-22)*: "Let us condemn him to a shameful death." In the gospel *(Jn 7:1-2, 10, 25-30)*, Jesus again makes his great claim, and we are told that "they would have arrested him, but because his time had not yet come no one laid a hand upon him." His time had not yet come but was now imminent.

While the gospels describe the outward scene, other readings give us insights into what took place within the mind and heart of Christ. Here the Church makes use of Old Testament prophecies and the psalms and does so to great effect. For example, on Saturday of the fourth week Christ's attitude of total trust in the Father is admirably expressed in the words of Jeremiah *(11:18-20)*: "I for my part was like a trustful lamb being led to the slaughter-house, not knowing the schemes they were plotting against me."

The word "trustful" is the key to his feelings. He accepts his Father's will unconditionally and with total trust. The psalms, with their constant note of trust in all human circumstances, are suitable for expressing the feelings of Christ on the eve of his passion. Take, for example, Psalm 7 which is used as a responsorial psalm during this time: "Lord, God, I take refuge in you. From my pursuer save me and rescue me:" and then the note of confidence: "God is the shield that protects me, who saves the upright of heart."

## The imitation of Christ

The passion of Christ is not just an object of con-
templation, but also a programme of Christian
living. It is summed up in those words of the Lord:
"If anyone wants to be a follower of mine, let him
renounce himself and take up his cross and follow
me" *(Mt 12:24)*. This call to renunciation is
repeated again and again in the New Testament
writings, as for example in the first letter of Peter
(*2:21*, RSV version): "For to this you have been
called, because Christ also suffered for you, leaving
for you an example, that you should follow in his
steps."

The office of readings is especially rich in this
regard. The patristic readings show us how the great
fathers of the Church have understood and
expanded upon this idea of the *imitatio Christi*.
The first father I would cite is St Augustine in his
commentary on Psalm 140, read on Tuesday of the
second week (*Divine Office* II, pp. 128-29). He
shows how Christ must continue to suffer in his
Church until the end of time. St Paul was of course
very conscious of the Church's participation in the
sufferings of Christ, especially in his own life. It is
a very basic message of Christian morality.

St Gregory the Great, in his commentary on the
book of Job, read on Friday of the third week
(*Divine Office* II, p. 167) has this to say: "If the
mystery of the Lord's passion is to be effectual in
us, we must imitate what we receive and proclaim
to others what we venerate." Again there is the
idea of imitation, the following of Christ even in

his passion. And this imitation or following must be motivated by love: "If you love, then follow", says Augustine in his homily for Sunday of the fourth week (p. 173).

The fathers of the eastern church express this idea of imitation in a more forceful and dramatic way. On Saturday of the fifth week we are addressed by St Gregory Nazianzen (*Divine Office* II, p. 247): "Let us accept everything literally, let us imitate the passion by our sufferings, let us reverence the blood by our blood, let us be eager to climb the cross." St Andrew of Crete also urges us to imitate Christ in his passion in the reading for Palm Sunday (p. 255): "Come, then, let us run with him as he presses on to his passion. Let us imitate those who have gone out to meet him, not scattering olive branches or garments or palms in his path, but spreading ourselves before him as best we can, with humility of soul and upright purpose."

Finally, there is that splendid prayer for Palm Sunday:

> Almight, ever-living God,
> you gave our Saviour the command
> to become man and undergo the cross,
> as an example of humility for all men to follow.
> We have the lessons of his sufferings;
> give us also the fellowship of his resurrection
> (*Breviary* version).

## The fruits of the passion

The mystery of the cross is a mystery of love and of unity: "And when I am lifted up from the earth, I shall draw all men to myself" *(Jn 12:32)*. Let us examine this and other fruits of Christ's saving passion in the light of the Lenten liturgy.

In the Mass lectionary we meet the theme of reconciliation on Ash Wednesday, in that great passage from St Paul *(2 Cor 5:20—6:2)*, in which he urges us to be "reconciled to God". Reconciliation is surely a key concept of Lent; it underlies our whole theology of penance. Reconciliation with God is possible because Christ, by his passion and death, has reconciled us with the Father. On the fourth Sunday of Lent (Year C) this message is repeated in the second reading *(2 Cor 5:17-21)*:

> It is all God's work. It was God who reconciled us with himself through Christ and gave us the work of handing on this reconciliation. In other words, God in Christ was reconciling the world to himself, not holding men's faults against them, and he has entrusted to us the news that they are reconciled.

Reconciliation is a strong term. It implies that there has been a break-down in human relations, that some serious rift has arisen between people as, for example, between married partners or members of a family or sections of a community. By becoming reconciled, the former happy relationship is restored. Something similar occurred between God and his creatures. Sin brought about a rift in man's relations with God. It produced division and estrangement, it destroyed the bond of friendship and intimacy between the two. Christ, the Son of God, came to repair what had been destroyed, to reconcile what had become estranged, to restore peace by his death on the cross.

We know how much Christ longed for unity, unity between the Father and his wayward children, unity among his followers, unity between Jew and Gentile, unity within the whole human family. In his great prayer at the Last Supper, he prayed "that they all may be one", but he knew that he would achieve that unity only by the sacrifice of his life. Caiphas, the high priest, unwittingly prophesied that Christ would die for the people, "and not for the nation only but to gather in unity the scattered children of God" (*Jn 11:52;* see also the gospel for Saturday of the fifth week).

By his life and death Christ atoned for our sins. It is significant that the word atonement derives from the three words "at-one-ment". From whatever angle we consider the saving work of Christ, unity is its ultimate effect; and this unity has its source in God's love. It is all part of God's eternal plan; it is brought about by the saving work of Christ and perfected by the sending of the Holy Spirit at Pentecost.

In the office of readings for Thursday of the fifth week (*Divine Office* II, pp. 231-32), our attention is drawn to the teaching of the Second Vatican Council. In its Constitution on the Church it has this to say:

> God has called together as one all who in faith look upon Jesus as the author of salvation and the source of unity and peace. He has established them as the Church, so that for each and all she may be the visible sacrament of this saving unity.

If our faith is strong, we shall draw from the cross of Christ all its inherent power. The Mass texts for Tuesday of the fifth week illustrate this. Here the image of the "fiery serpent" helps us to understand the healing and redeeming power of the cross. (See first reading, *Nb 21:4-9.*) The bronze serpent was placed on a standard, and simply by looking up at it people were healed of their snake bites. For the Church fathers it was a figure of the passion of Christ; it foretold the saving power of the cross. The gospel of that day *(Jn 8:21-30)* perfectly matches this Old Testament reading. In it Jesus, speaking of his own death on the cross, seems to allude to the episode of the bronze serpent. His words are prophetic: "When you have lifted up the Son of Man then you will know that I am he." The cross is a healing power; to look up at Christ with faith is to be saved.

# 5   Introducing Holy Week

Of all the weeks in the year Holy Week is the one most revered by Christians. It has been hallowed by the events which we commemorate in the liturgy and in a very special way has been consecrated to God. The Church, in celebrating the passion, death and resurrection of Christ, sanctifies and renews herself.

This week was also known in ancient times as "The Great Week", a title which was retained until recently in the old Roman breviary.[1] It is indeed a great week since it constitutes the heart and kernel of the liturgical year. It celebrates the mystery of redemption. The Christians of antiquity had no doubt about its greatness; one early writer summed it up in the revealing phrase: "Easter is the summit."

One of the most penetrating commentaries on Holy Week is that of the German Benedictine nun, Aemiliana Löhr, significantly entitled *The Great Week*.[2] It is full of revealing insights and arresting thoughts, one of which can be of particular help to us in this introductory section. This is that we should enter Holy Week in a spirit of inner peace and recollectedness. We know from experience that these last days before Easter can be a time of frenetic activity; we often get carried away with

48

last-minute preparations for the feast of Easter,
and leave the fulfilling of our spiritual obligations
to one last great effort.

Aemiliana Löhr, in her first chapter (pp.12-14),
uses the beautiful image of a ship entering port after
a long voyage. It is an image of peace: the weeks of
effort and strain are over. The Church is like that
ship. Lent has been a long voyage, a time of labour
and self-discipline, but now in Holy Week the
Church has entered port; it is time to rest in the
passion of Christ. It may not be easy to take time
off for God, but this idea of resting in the passion
suggests the attitude of mind we should have in
approaching Holy Week.

We could rest in the thought of God's love
which is at the origin of all the events we commemorate in this week: "Yes, God loved the world so
much that he gave his only Son" *(Jn 3:16)*. The
whole passion was motivated by love, the love of
God made visible in Christ. Again it is John who
tells us: "He had always loved those who were his
in the world, but now he showed how perfect his
love was" *(Jn 13:1)*.

During Holy Week the Church follows in the
footsteps of the Master. The passion narrative
comes to life as though it were being re-enacted
before our eyes. All the events leading up to the
arrest, trial and execution of Jesus are recalled and
celebrated. Step by step, scene by scene, we follow
along the path which Christ trod during the last
days of his mortal life.

The Holy Week liturgy grew out of the devotion
of the early Christians[3] in Jerusalem where Jesus

endured his passion. Jerusalem, from very early times, became a place of pilgrimage; and pilgrims, then as now, loved to visit the sites of the passion— Gethsemane, the Pretorium, Golgatha, the holy sepulchre. One of the most interesting documents which have come down to us from early times is the travel-diary of the Spanish pilgrim Egeria.[4] It gives us a most graphic account of the Holy Week liturgy as celebrated in Jerusalem about the year 400 A. D.

We have much to learn from the devotion of the ancient Church, as witnessed to in the writings which have survived. It is true that the Christians of Jerusalem had an advantage over us: they were closer to our Lord both in time and place. But our devotion need not be any less. After all, we share in the mysteries of Christ, not through imagination or feeling, though these have their role, but through faith. In the liturgy of Holy Week the Church re- lives in faith the saving mysteries of the passion, death and resurrection of the Lord.

# 6    Passion or Palm Sunday

Passion Sunday, or Palm Sunday as it is more popularly known, inaugurates Holy Week. According to a rubrical note, "On this day the Church celebrates Christ's entrance into Jerusalem to accomplish his paschal mystery." All four evangelists record this event and underline its importance. Jesus is presented as the Messiah-King, entering and taking possession of his city. He comes, however, not as a warrior-king advancing with a great army, but as a humble and gentle Messiah. He fulfils the prophecy of Zechariah (Zc 9:9): "Lo, your king comes to you; triumphant and victorious is he, humble and riding on an ass."

## The procession

The procession is characterised by joy, a joy that anticipates that of Easter. It is a procession in honour of Christ the King; that is the reason for the red vestments, the acclamations and hymns in honour of Christ the King. The Church re-enacts the events of the first Palm Sunday: what we read in the gospel comes to life in the procession.[1]

The procession is not just pageantry. It is something very real; in a sense it is even more real than

51

the original event itself for the Church, in celebrating this event with faith and devotion, is celebrating the mystery hidden within it. The king we acclaim is not just a figure of history, but one who lives and reigns now and forever. The significance of Christ's triumphal entry is perceived only by those who have faith. He enters "to complete his work as our Messiah, to suffer, to die and to rise again".

"Blessed is he who comes in the name of the Lord, hosanna in the highest!" We hear this acclamation at every Mass, at the beginning of the eucharistic prayer. Christ's coming in the eucharistic mystery is a daily happening. In the Palm Sunday procession the Church, represented in each liturgical assembly, goes out to meet and to welcome Christ in a special way.

The procession gives us a kind of preview or foretaste of Easter Sunday. The joy and triumph of Easter breaks through the otherwise sombre liturgy of this day. The palms, which are blessed and carried in procession, are an emblem of victory: "Today we honour Christ our triumphant King by carrying these branches." The resurrection is explicitly mentioned in the responsory sung as the procession enters the Church: "The children of Jerusalem welcomed Christ the King. They proclaimed the resurrection of life."

In the Palm Sunday procession the Church not only commemorates a past event and celebrates a present reality, but also anticipates its final accomplishment. The Church looks forward to the fulfilment of the mystery at the end of time. This eschatological note is sounded in the prayer said at the blessing of the palm branches: "Today we joyfully acclaim Jesus our Messiah and King. May we reach one day the happiness of the new and everlasting Jerusalem." One of the petitions for the morning office, addressed to Christ, also has this note of longing for future fulfilment: "You went up to Jerusalem to endure the passion and enter into glory; lead your Church into the paschal feast of eternal life."

## Liturgy of the Word

The day is called both Palm Sunday and Passion Sunday: the palm for victory and the passion for suffering. The procession heralds the victory of Easter Sunday; in contrast to this, the Liturgy of the Word which follows plunges us into the atmosphere of Good Friday. Christ will indeed conquer, but it will be through his passion and death.[2]

The first reading is from the prophet Isaiah *(50: 4-7)*. The prophet's sufferings at the hands of his enemies prefigure those of Christ. His calm acceptance of insult and injury makes us think of Christ's humility under even greater provocation. It is suffering freely accepted and willingly endured. We meet this idea of voluntary acceptance again in the second reading *(Ph 2:6-11)*, where we are told: "He (Christ) was humbler yet, even to accepting death, death on a cross." It is also the theme of the preface: "Though he was sinless, he suffered willingly for sinners; though innocent, he accepted death to save the guilty."

The second reading gives us a profound insight into the mystery of redemption. St Paul, addressing the Philippians, speaks of the self-emptying *(kenosis)* of Christ. He not only "emptied himself to assume the condition of a slave" but humbled himself even to accepting death on a cross. This was the ultimate in humility and abasement, to become an outcast, one rejected by society. But St Paul, having sounded the depths of Christ's sufferings, immediately directs our thoughts upwards: "But God raised him high and gave him the name which is above all other names."

The solemn reading of the passion narrative is the most characteristic feature of the Mass. According to the three-year cycle, the gospel account is that of Matthew, Mark or Luke. Traditionally, it is the passion according to St Matthew which is read this day.

The reading of the gospel is stripped of the usual ceremonial, even at a high Mass: no lights, or incense, even the sign of the cross is omitted at the beginning. It begins with the bare announcement: "The passion of our Lord Jesus Christ according to Matthew". The gospel of the passion needs no adornment; it does not even require an introduction or homily; it speaks for itself. When read with reverence it cannot fail to make a deep impression.

There are many books on the life of Christ, many meditations and tracts on the passion. Nothing makes a greater impact on us, however, than the sober but poignant accounts of the Lord's passion given us by the evangelists themselves. Here no attempt is made to play on our feelings or to pre-

sent a highly coloured account of what happened.
Neither do we detect any playing down of the suffering, physical and moral, endured by our Lord. It
is a story simply told, with dignity and restraint.
And yet it tells all, so much so that we may well
imagine that we are witnessing these events. There
is drama and pathos but also serenity. The figure of
Christ towers above his accusers and persecutors.

The custom of employing three readers for the
gospel is a good one. This helps to sustain attention
and interest. It also highlights the words of Christ,
a role fittingly played by the celebrant himself. A
second reader will act as a narrator and a third will
assume the other parts.

# 7 Monday to Wednesday

No special celebrations mark the first half of Holy Week. During these days the Church ponders deeply on the mystery of the Lord's passion, as witness the texts of the missal, lectionary and breviary. To read and reflect on these texts is to acquire the authentic spirit of Holy Week. It is to "rest in the passion of Christ".

In the office of readings the Letter to the Hebrews, begun on Sunday of the fifth week, continues to be read. This reveals the deep significance and redemptive value of Christ's sufferings. Here Christ is presented in his dual role of priest and victim. The efficacy of his sacrifice is declared unequivocally: "By virtue of that one single offering, he has achieved the eternal perfection of all whom he is sanctifying" *(Heb 10:13)*.

The theme of the "imitation of Christ", already commented on in the Lenten liturgy, recurs here. It finds expression in the patristic readings of the morning office. What Christ endured for our sakes is shown as the pattern of Christian living. Thus, St Basil, in the reading for Tuesday, has this to say:

> So, for perfection of life it is necessary not only to imitate Christ, in the examples of

gentleness, and humility, and patience which he gave us in his life, but also to imitate him in his death, as Paul the imitator of Christ says: "Becoming like him in his death, that if possible I may attain the resurrection from the dead" (*Divine Office* II, p. 270).

St Augustine also broaches this theme of imitation in his homily for Wednesday (*ibid.*, pp. 276-78). It is a homily on the fullness of Christian love as exemplified by Christ when he laid down his life for us. We must imitate his example, and like the martyrs, be ready to lay down our lives for our brethren. St Augustine concludes: "So let us love one another as Christ loved us and gave himself for us."

On Spy Wednesday as it is called the betrayal by Judas is introduced. The gospel *(Mt 26:14-25)* describes how Judas went to the chief priests and offered to betray Jesus for thirty pieces of silver. With this act of treachery on the part of a trusted disciple of the Lord the hour of darkness is at hand.

# 8  The Easter triduum

The word triduum in Catholic devotional practice suggests the idea of preparation. We may, for example, prepare for the feast of a saint by observing three days of prayer in that saint's honour; or we may seek to obtain some special favour by holding a triduum of prayer and intercession.

The Easter or paschal triduum was seen as a three-days' preparation for the feast of Easter. It comprised Thursday, Friday and Saturday of Holy Week. It was a triduum of the passion.

In the new Calendar and reformed Order of Holy Week, a shift of emphasis has taken place. The triduum is presented not just as a period of preparation but as a unified whole. It is a triduum of the passion and resurrection; it embraces the whole celebration of the paschal mystery. This is what the Calendar says:

> Christ redeemed mankind and gave perfect glory to God principally through his paschal mystery: by dying he destroyed our death and by rising he restored our life. The Easter triduum of the passion and resurrection of Christ is thus the culmination of the entire liturgical year.

It then goes on to determine the exact duration of

the triduum:

> The Easter triduum begins with the evening Mass of the Lord's supper, reaches its high point in the Easter Vigil and closes with Vespers on Easter Sunday.

This unifying of the Easter celebration is closer to the spirit of the New Testament and of early Christian tradition. Christ himself, in alluding to his passion and death, did not disassociate these from his resurrection. In the gospel for Wednesday of the second week of Lent *(Mt 20:17-28)* he speaks of them conjointly: "They will condemn him to death and will hand him over to the pagans to be mocked and scourged and crucified; and on the third day he will rise again."

It is significant that among the Church fathers both St Ambrose and St Augustine conceive the Easter triduum as a unity embracing both the suffering and glorification of Jesus. Thus the Bishop of Milan, in one of his writings, refers to the three holy days (*triduum illud sacrum*) as the three days "within which he suffered, lay in the tomb, and arose, the three days of which he said: 'Destroy this temple and in three days I will raise it up'".[1] St Augustine, in one of his letters, refers to "the three most sacred days of his (Christ's) crucifixion, burial and resurrection".[2]

These three days, beginning with the evening Mass on Holy Thursday and concluding with evening prayer on Easter Sunday, form a unity and should be viewed as such. It follows that Easter, the Christian pasch, consists essentially of a three-

day celebration; it embraces both the dark and
radiant sides of Christ's saving mystery. Spread
over these three days are the different phases of
the Easter mystery. The Easter triduum may be
likened to a triptych: three pictures, each depicting
a part of the scene, together forming a unity; each
picture is complete but needs to be viewed in
relation to the other two.

Of interest in this connection is the fact that
Good Friday and Holy Saturday do not officially
belong to the season of Lent. According to the new
Calendar, Lent begins on Ash Wednesday and is
concluded on Holy Thursday, exclusive of the Mass
of the Lord's Supper.[3] Friday and Saturday of
Holy Week are not the last two days of Lent, but
the first two days of "the most sacred triduum".

## Thoughts for the triduum

The unity of the paschal mystery has something
important to teach us. It teaches us that sorrow is
not simply followed by joy, but that it already
contains joy. Jesus used many images to express
this; for instance, at the Last Supper he told his
apostles: "You will be sorrowful, but your sorrow
will turn to joy" (Jn 16:20). It is as though sorrow
were one of the ingredients from which joy would
be fashioned. The image of a woman in the pains
of childbirth beautifully expresses this. Her pain
actually generates joy, the joy "that a man has
been born into the world".

Other images also come to mind. The whole
cycle of nature speaks of life out of death: "Unless

# THE EASTER TRIDUUM 61

a wheat grain falls on the ground and dies, it remains only a single grain; but if it dies, it yields a rich harvest" *(Jn 12:24)*.

Easter is our passover; it is a passing over from death to life, from darkness to light, from fast to feast. Our Lord said: "But when you fast, put oil on your head and wash your face" *(Mt 6:17)*. The fast is the beginning of the feast.

Suffering is not a good thing in itself and so is not to be sought after for its own sake. The Christian approach to it is positive and realistic. In the life of Christ, and above all in the cross, we see its redemptive value. The crucifix can never be just a painful reminder of what Christ suffered for us. It is an object in which we can glory because it is transfigured by the glory of the resurrection.

In our own lives joy and sorrow intermingle. To shrink from pain and sorrow at all costs and to seek joy and pleasure for their own sakes are both mistaken attitudes. The Christian way is the way illuminated by the teaching and example of Christ. It is the way of the cross which is also the way of the resurrection; it is self-forgetfulness, it is losing oneself for Christ's sake, it is life out of death. The paschal mystery, which we celebrate during these days of the triduum, is the pattern and the programme our own lives should follow.

# 9 Holy Thursday

Holy Thursday stands at the cross roads between Lent and Easter. It is the last day of Lent and its evening Mass ushers in the paschal triduum. It is the final preparation for Easter and already initiates the Easter celebration.

Preparation is the key word for this day. Everything is made in readiness for the pasch. So it was with the first Holy Thursday when the Lord sent Peter and John to make preparations: "Go and make the preparations for us to eat the passover" *(Lk 22:8)*

For the faithful it is a day of spiritual preparation. In ancient times the public penitents were reconciled with the Church on this day; in a solemn and public rite they were received back into full communion with the Church; absolved from their sins, they could now celebrate the pasch and receive their paschal communion with the rest of the faithful. It would be in line with Christian tradition to make our Easter confession on this day, if we have not already done so.

Two Masses are celebrated on this day, one in the cathedral churches only (the Chrism Mass) and the other (Evening Mass of the Lord's Supper) in parish churches and churches of religious orders.

The Chrism Mass includes the blessing of the oils needed for baptism and other sacraments. Here the emphasis is on the theme of priesthood and its institution by Christ. The evening Mass commemorates more specifically the institution of the eucharist. The two themes are intimately connected, but it helps us to distinguish them by having two celebrations.

## The Chrism Mass

As mentioned above the Chrism Mass is celebrated only in cathedral churches. It takes place in the morning, the diocesan bishop acting as consecrator of the oils and as chief concelebrant. It is an impressive and beautiful rite and is catechetically very rich.

In this coming together of the people of God we have a very expressive manifestation of the Church, for the diocese is the Church of God in miniature. In ancient times it was possible for a bishop to celebrate the eucharist surrounded by almost his entire flock. This is hardly feasible today, yet it remains the ideal. This ideal is well expressed in the Liturgy Constitution of Vatican II:

> They (the faithful) must be convinced that the pre-eminent manifestation of the Church consists in the full, active participation of all God's holy people in these liturgical celebrations, especially in the same eucharist, in a single prayer, at one altar, at which the bishop presides surrounded by his college of priests and ministers (41).

The Holy Thursday liturgy in the cathedral comes very close to this ideal. Here we have the bishop, head of the local church, surrounded by priests from all the parishes of his diocese and by priests representing the religious orders. The bishop concelebrates Mass with his priests as a sign of unity and fellowship. He is assisted by them in the blessing of the oils. The deacons and other ministers are also present and take an active part.

As a visible expression of the hierarchical Church this occasion is almost unique. It is all the more so if the faithful of the diocese are there in large numbers. Their presence and participation is greatly desired, for the Church is incomplete if it does not include the lay people of God. Those of the faithful who attend may receive communion at the Chrism Mass and again in the evening.

It is significant that the oils for use in the sacraments are blessed within the context of the eucharist and in close proximity to Easter. This is not by accident. The sacraments derive their meaning and efficacy from the paschal mystery of Christ. This mystery is renewed in each eucharistic celebration and with special solemnity in the paschal feast. To quote again from the Liturgy Constitution:

> Thus for well-disposed members of the faithful the liturgy of the sacraments and the sacramentals sanctifies almost every event of their lives with the divine grace which flows from the paschal mystery of the passion, death and resurrection of Christ. From this source all sacraments and sacramentals draw their power (61).

All the sacraments have a connection with Easter; they are *paschal* sacraments. We might remind ourselves of this when we assist at a baptism, confirmation or ordination and the holy oil of chrism is used; or when someone is anointed with the oil of the sick.

The priesthood is the major theme of the Chrism Mass. In bequeathing the mystery of the eucharist to the Church, Christ also instituted the Christian priesthood. The texts of the Mass present a catechesis of the priesthood, referring not only to the ministerial priesthood but also to the general priesthood of the faithful. Thus in the entrance antiphon the assembly acclaims: "Jesus Christ has made us a kingdom of priests to serve his God and Father." This is repeated in the second reading and is echoed in the preface.

All priesthood is a sharing in the one priesthood of Christ. He is our Mediator and High Priest. His anointing is from the Holy Spirit. This is brought out in the reading from Isaiah *(61:1-3, 6, 8-9)* and in the gospel from Luke *(4:16-21)*, in which our Lord quotes and applies to himself the prophetic texts: "The spirit of the Lord has been given to me, for he has anointed me."

Through the sacrament of holy orders men share in a unique way in the priesthood of Christ: to them alone is given the power to remit sins and to change bread and wine into the body and blood of Christ; they do this in the name and through the power of Christ. They are in a special way pastors and teachers of the Church, as well as administrators of the sacraments. All this is summed up in the preface:

> He appoints them to renew in his name the sacrifice of our redemption as they set before your family his paschal meal. He calls them to lead your holy people in love, nourish them by your word, and strengthen them through the sacraments.

It is not easy for the priest to live up to the demands of his vocation and ministry. He needs the prayer and support of his fellow Christians. He needs from time to time to "fan into a flame" the gift that God gave him *(2 Tm 1:6)*.

One of the most impressive features of the Chrism Mass, and a recent addition, is the renewal of commitment to priestly service. After the gospel and homily the bishop invites his priests to renew their dedication to Christ and his Church. Together they solemnly undertake to unite themselves more closely to Christ, to be his faithful ministers, to teach and to offer the holy sacrifice in his name, to lead and guide others to him.

In this act of commitment the bishop asks for himself the prayers of all his people. He needs their prayers. As that great bishop, St Augustine, once said to his people: "While I am frightened by what I am to you, I am also consoled by what I share with you. For you I am a bishop, with you I am a Christian."[1]

In a very real way a bishop represents Christ in his diocese: "The bishop is to be considered as the High Priest of his flock from whom the life in Christ of his faithful is in some way derived and upon whom it in some way depends" (Liturgy Constitution, 41).

The blessing of the oils and consecration of the chrism may take place after the renewal of commitment or at a later point in the Mass. The older tradition places the blessing of the oil of the sick just before the end of the eucharistic prayer; the blessing of the oil of catechumens and the consecration of the chrism is of special interest. All the concelebrating priests associate themselves with the consecratory prayer, which is one of the most solemn in the liturgy. It provides an effective lesson on the dignity and power of the sacraments, especially the sacrament of baptism.

## Evening Mass of the Lord's Supper

The evening Mass commemorates the Last Supper and the institution of the eucharist. Everything seems to evoke the memory of that paschal meal which Christ shared with his disciples: the time (late evening), the recalling in the readings of the institution of the eucharist, Christ's final discourse and the washing of the disciples' feet; the insertion into the eucharistic prayer of the words: "The day before he suffered to save us and all men, that is today, he took bread in his sacred hands". . . .

It was in the course of this meal that our Lord founded his own memorial, the eucharist:

At the Last Supper, on the night he was betrayed, our Saviour instituted the eucharistic sacrifice of his body and blood. This he did in order to perpetuate the sacrifice of the Cross throughout the ages until he should come again, and so to entrust to his beloved spouse, the Church, a memorial of his death and resurrection: a sacrament of love, a sign of unity, a bond of charity, a paschal banquet in which Christ is consumed, the mind is filled with grace, and a pledge of future glory is given to us.[2]

"A sacrament of love, a sign of unity, a bond of charity"—that is what the eucharist was intended to be; and on this evening it reveals itself very clearly in that light. What could be more expressive of unity than a meal shared among a family or among friends? The eucharist is a meal, Christ is our host, the altar a table and we are God's family. The Mass is not only a sacred meal, but that is the aspect of the eucharistic mystery which is highlighted this evening. It is under the symbolism of a sacred meal that we discover the community dimension of the Mass.

A spirit of joy characterises the Mass. It is a deep, interior joy; it is the joy which Christ experienced in his own soul on this occasion. He had looked forward to it: "I have longed and longed to share this paschal meal with you." In that final discourse, recorded by John (13–17), the word joy occurs very frequently. For every Jewish family the passover meal was a time of great family joy; it was an event eagerly awaited. Christ would have experienced this joy, but his joy went much deeper. His was the joy of total sacrifice, the joy of one who gives without counting the cost. Christ rejoices in the fulfilment of his Father's will of which he is the perfect human instrument.

This joy is given liturgical expression in the Mass. The chants are joyful, the *Gloria* is sung or recited (in some places to the accompaniment of bells), and white vestments are worn. Everything suggests joy and festivity. Only the *Alleluia* is absent. This is to remind us that it is not yet Easter Sunday.

The entrance antiphon sounds a triumphal note: "It is our duty to glory in the cross of our Lord Jesus Christ. He saves us and sets us free; through him we find salvation, life and resurrection." It is very impressive when this is sung as celebrant and ministers approach the altar preceded by the processional cross, the emblem of victory.

The eucharist is Christ's own memorial of his sacrifice on the cross. There is an intimate and necessary connection between the Mass and Calvary. What our Lord does at the Last Supper, and commands his disciples to do in memory of him, announces and anticipates his self-oblation on Good Friday. It is significant that in Jerusalem on this day the holy sacrifice was offered "behind the cross", that is at Golgatha.[3]

The opening prayer declares that Christ gave us this sacrament to reveal his love, and goes on to ask that in it we may find the fullness of love and life.

The first reading *(Ex 12:1-8, 11-14)* gives the Old Testament instructions concerning the passover meal. It prefigures the passover of Christ and the paschal banquet which he will institute. By instituting the eucharist and undergoing his passion in the course of the paschal celebrations, Christ intended to show that he was the fulfilment of the Old Testament figures, that he was the true lamb, slain in sacrifice, whose blood would save his people. In the course of the paschal meal he changed bread and wine into his body and blood, thus establishing the paschal rite of the Church.

The second reading (*1 Cor 11:23-26*) gives us St Paul's account of the Last Supper and the institution of the eucharist. It is clear that at the time he was writing (about 57 A. D.) the liturgical tradition was firmly established. As this may be the earliest account of the institution it is of particular interest and value. It witnesses to the faith of the primitive Church in the Real Presence, the sacrificial character of the eucharist ("This is my body, which is for you") and its awareness that in celebrating the eucharist it is fulfilling the Lord's command: "Do this as a memorial of me." It also shows that the eucharist is both memorial and promise, that it not only constitutes Christ's memorial (*anamnesis*) but also heralds his return at the end of time.

The gospel (*Jn 13:1-15*) describes the washing of the disciples' feet. It is well chosen to illustrate the theme of fraternal love. The eucharist is the sacrament of love: it commits us to a life of love and service. Christ taught the doctrine of love by his whole life. At the Last Supper he repeats and develops his teaching, and reinforces his words by symbolic action. The gesture of the washing of the feet puzzled and astonished the apostles; but, in a way that no words could, it drove home the lesson of mutual love and service: "I have given you an example so that you may copy what I have done to you."

The liturgy has preserved for optional use the

medieval rite of the washing of feet. After the
gospel and homily the celebrant puts on an apron
and takes a towel. Twelve men, representing the
apostles, come forward and take their places in
front of the sanctuary. The priest goes to each man,
pours water over his feet and dries them. As the
gospel scene is thus re-enacted the choir may sing
some of the traditional antiphons, made up of sen-
tences from St John, such as: "I give you a new
commandment: love one another as I have loved
you." This miming of the gospel is a kind of audio-
visual aid. It may strike us as rather strange but in
the time of our Lord there was nothing strange
about washing the feet of guests; it was a simple
gesture of hospitality. Performed by Christ at the
Last Supper it had a much deeper significance.[1] It
conveyed, first of all, the message of mutual service;
authority must be understood and practised as a
form of service. Here Christ has given the perfect
example. At a deeper level, Christ in this gesture is
prophesying his own death. The washing of the disciples' feet symbolised the supreme act of loving
service for mankind, Christ's atoning sacrifice. Its
message is that not only should we imitate Christ's
spirit of service in little things, but be prepared to
follow him all the way even, if necessary, to the
extent of laying down our lives.

The liturgy of the eucharist now begins. At the
presentation of gifts (Offertory) the idea of service,
in this case service of the poor, is again to the fore.
It is customary at this Mass to have a collection for
the poor; and at this point of the celebration, gifts
for the poor, in money or in kind, are brought in

procession to the altar together with the bread and wine. During the procession an appropriate hymn is sung. The traditional hymn of fraternal love *Ubi caritas et amor, Deus ibi est* (Where charity and love are found, there is God) is very appropriate.

The preface is that of the Holy Eucharist. If Eucharistic Prayer I is employed, as seems appropriate, the ancient text is suitably adapted to fit this particular occasion: "Father, accept this offering from your whole family in memory of the day when Jesus Christ, our Lord, gave the mysteries of his body and blood for his disciples to celebrate."

At communion time an extraordinary impression of unity is created. There are no private Masses and only one eucharistic celebration in each church apart from cathedrals. The local community, young and old, priests and laity, gather round a single altar, and the clergy of the parish or religious community concelebrate or simply receive communion. In this way the unity of the Church, the body of Christ, is highlighted: a unity strengthened and sustained by the eucharist, the sacrament of love.

After the distribution of communion, the ciborium with hosts for Good Friday is left on the altar, and Mass concludes with the prayer after communion. After Mass the priest, accompanied by his ministers, carries the blessed sacrament in procession to the altar of repose. This solemn procession with lights and incense and the singing of the *Pange lingua* evokes the feast of the Body and Blood of Christ. It brings out another dimension of the eucharist, that of permanent sacrament. In the words of Pope Paul VI: "It is not only while the sacrifice is being offered and the sacrament is being constituted that Christ is truly Emmanuel, 'God with us'; for day and night he is in our midst, dwelling among us full of grace and truth."[5]

The Holy Thursday liturgy is over, but not personal prayer and devotion. The faithful are encouraged to continue adoration at the altar of repose for a suitable time between now and midnight. This is a kind of private vigil which commemorates Christ's own vigil in the garden of Gethsemane when he was overcome with sorrow. We are reminded of our Lord's words to the three disciples: "Wait here and keep awake with me" and "So you had not the strength to keep awake with me one hour" *(Mt 26:38-41).*

# 10 Good Friday

Good Friday is a day of intense sorrow, but of sorrow sweetened by Christian hope. The remembrance of what Christ suffered for us cannot fail to arouse in us feelings of sorrow and compassion, and of regret for our share in the sins of the world.

Devotion to the passion of Christ is deep-rooted in Christian piety. It is witnessed to in the early Church and, indeed, in the New Testament writings. The pilgrim, Egeria, describing the Good Friday ceremonies in Jerusalem in 400 A. D., has left us a vivid and moving account of the people's reaction to the passion readings: "It is impressive to see the way the people are moved by these readings, and how they mourn. You could hardly believe how every single one of them weeps during these three hours, old and young alike, because of the manner in which the Lord suffered for us."[1]

The Good Friday liturgy presents a synthesis of all that is best in devotion to the passion of Christ. The spirit of the early Church is there with its emphasis on the glory of the cross; also the realism, tenderness and compassion of the middle ages. The insights of every age, the piety of both western and eastern Christianity are somehow blended together to form one harmonious whole.

## Celebration of the Lord's passion

Celebration of the Lord's passion takes place in the afternoon, about three o'clock, the time when Jesus was crucified. As a general rule only one celebration is allowed in each church. In Ireland, because of the very large numbers who throng the churches on this day, a second celebration is allowed.[2]

The celebration falls into three parts: Liturgy of the Word; veneration of the cross; holy communion.

## Liturgy of the Word

The ceremony begins in a very simple way. The celebrant and ministers approach the altar in silence. There they make a reverence or, according to the ancient manner, prostrate themselves. All pray in silence for a little while. The priest then reads the opening prayer after which all sit down to listen to the readings.

The first reading (*Isaiah 52:13—53:12*) presents us with the "suffering servant", a prophetic figure in whom Christian tradition, and the New Testament itself, has recognised Christ.[3] Christ in his passion is indeed the "man of sorrows" so powerfully portrayed in this poem. It is all there: his sufferings and humiliations, his rejection by his people, his atoning death; even the details of the passion narrative are there, e. g. "He was pierced through for our faults."

This passage sets the tone for the Good Friday service. Yet even here the darkness is shot through with light and hope. The very first line of the poem points to ultimate victory: "See, my servant will prosper, he shall be lifted up, exalted, rise to great heights." It is with this note of exaltation that the poem is concluded. Because God's servant accepts his role of expiatory victim, he brings peace, healing and justification to many: "His soul's anguish over, he shall see the light and be content. By his sufferings shall my servant justify many, taking their faults on himself."

The second reading *(Heb 4:14-16; 5:7-9)* presents Christ in his priestly role, reconciling men to God through the sacrifice of his own life.[4] He is both priest and victim, offerer and offered; he is our mediator with the Father. In this reading we contemplate Christ in his heavenly existence and in his present activity. In the gospel we have the record of his suffering and death.

Christ is not a figure of the past, nor is he a remote, impassive personage. He has experienced our human lot in every way, sin excepted. He can therefore sympathise with us in our sorrow and wretchedness, because he too has suffered in his sacred humanity.

## The gospel

"The passion of our Lord Jesus Christ according to John." With this simple introduction the reader begins the Good Friday gospel *(Jn 18:1–19:42)*. It seems to have always been the tradition of the Roman Church that it is the passion narrative of St John that is read on this day. St John, the theologian and mystic, views the passion of Jesus more

profoundly than the other evangelists, in the light
of the resurrection. His Easter faith transfigures
each detail and episode of this last phase of our
Lord's earthly life.[5]

Take, for example, the treatment of the cross in
St John. In itself it is something cruel and barbarous;
but since Christ redeemed mankind by the wood of
the cross it is an object of veneration. It is more
than that. For St John the cross is a kind of throne.
The raising of Jesus on the cross is described as an
"exaltation", a term which suggests at once the
idea of being lifted up and glorified. It is St John
who tells us that Jesus bore his own cross. . . .

The sufferings of our Lord are not minimised,
and yet an atmosphere of peace and serenity pervades the whole account. It is Christ, not his persecutors, who is in control of the situation. There
is no constraint: he freely goes to his execution;
with perfect liberty and complete awareness of the
significance of the events, he goes to meet his fate.
The motive, the ultimate explanation, is love. The
cross is the supreme revelation of the love of God.

In the portrait given by St John Jesus appears in
a three-fold role: as king, judge and saviour. The
mockery of the soldiers and the crowning with
thorns only serve to underline his kingship. In the
very act of condemning him it is Jesus, not Pilate,
who is shown as judge; before his words and before
his cross we stand condemned or justified. Finally,
as saviour, Jesus gathers his people in unity around
his cross. The Church, represented by the seamless
robe, is formed. On Mary, his mother, is conferred
a spiritual maternity: she becomes mother of all

the living. From the cross Jesus renders up his
spirit, thus inaugurating the final period of salvation. From his pierced side flow blood and water,
symbols of salvation and of the life-giving Spirit.
Christ is shown as the true paschal lamb, whose
blood of old saved the Israelites. To look on him
with faith is to be saved.

## General intercessions

In the general intercessions we have a survival of an
ancient form of the prayer of the faithful. At one
time such solemn prayers of intercession appear to
have been a common feature of the Roman liturgy.[6]
In this extended and elaborate form they are retained only on this one day in the year. In the ten
great prayers of intercession the Church looks out
on the whole world and earnestly pleads on behalf
of all mankind.

This prayer is truly universal; it includes all cate-
gories of people. It is fitting that it should be so on
this day when Christian people everywhere are
gathered round the cross of Christ, associating
themselves with his priestly prayer. His prayer extended to all because his love included all. "For
our sake he opened his arms on the cross" in a gesture which embraced the whole world. The cross
on which he died is, in Christian tradition, a symbol
of universality: its four corners point to the four
corners of the world.

These ancient Good Friday prayers have been
adapted to present-day circumstances. They reflect
the ecumenical spirit of our day. There is no men-

tion now of heretics and schismatics but of "all our brothers and sisters who share our faith in Jesus Christ". That wider ecumenism which seeks closer ties of friendship with non-Christian religions is not lacking either. In the prayer for the Jewish people, for example, there is respect and love. They are referred to as "the first to hear the word of God", and we ask that they may grow in the love of God's name and in faithfulness to his covenant.

Two new prayers, very relevant to our time, have been added: "for those who do not believe in Christ", and "for those who do not believe in God". It is salutary to remember that Christians form only a small minority of the world's population: by comparison with the millions of non-Christians the Church of Christ is indeed "a little flock". The harvest is therefore very great, and we should pray "for those who do not believe in Christ, that the light of the Holy Spirit may show them the way to salvation".

The other prayer is for those who do not believe in God. Atheism is widespread today; science, technology, a materialistic philosophy and other factors have had an undermining effect on religious belief. In great areas of the world people live under regimes which are militantly anti-religious. There are parts of the world where the light of the Gospel can scarcely penetrate. But all, whether Christian or atheist, form part of the one human family. We pray for all our brothers and sisters outside the fold, that by living sincere and upright lives they may come to the knowledge of God.

Last of all, there is a prayer for those in special need: the sick, the dying, travellers, prisoners, etc. These general intercessions are truly universal. In this great exercise of intercession, in which all the faithful are actively engaged, the Church is most surely recognised in her role of *ecclesia orans*, "the praying Church".

## The veneration of the cross

The eucharistic sacrifice is not offered on Good Friday. The central part of the Mass, the eucharistic prayer, is missing. In its place we have the moving ceremony of the veneration of the cross. This is followed by a simple communion service.

The very absence of the eucharistic sacrifice this day brings home to us the intimate relationship between the sacrifice of Calvary and the Mass. Christ died once-for-all for our sins. His sacrifice is unique and all-sufficient. But the memorial of that death and sacrifice is celebrated at every Mass. In each celebration of the eucharist "the work of our redemption is renewed". On this day the Church's gaze is fixed on Calvary itself where Christ offered his life in atonement for our sins.

The rite of veneration has two forms. The celebrant will choose the form which he considers more suitable. The first form consists of a gradual unveiling of the cross. Standing at the altar, the priest uncovers the upper part of the cross, unveils it and says or sings: "This is the wood of the cross", to which the people reply: "Come, let us worship." They then kneel down and venerate the cross in

silence. There follows a second unveiling, that of
the right arm of the cross, and again the invitation
to worship. Finally the priest uncovers the entire
cross and there is a third veneration.

Although this first form has a long and interesting history, the second form seems more effective.
Here there is a solemn procession with the unveiled
cross from the church door to the sanctuary. The
cross is carried by the priest or deacon accompanied
by ministers with lighted candles. On the way to
the altar there are three "stations" during which
the cross is venerated. Near the entrance, in the
middle of the church and at the entrance to the
sanctuary, the priest or deacon carrying the cross
stops, lifts it up and says or sings: "This is the wood
of the cross"; the response and art of veneration
follow as above. The cross is now placed in position
at the entrance to the sanctuary so that all the
faithful may approach to venerate it either by a
genuflection or by kissing it.

Ideally everyone in the congregation should be
given the opportunity to pay personal homage to
the crucified Saviour. In the simple gesture of kissing the cross, popular piety expresses itself spon-
taneously and movingly. To the sombre and majes-
tic liturgy of this day, it introduces a personal and
tender note. The gesture of kissing the cross also
has a long history behind it: the Christians of Jerusalem venerated it in this way on Good Friday as
early as the fourth century.[7]

As the faithful approach to kiss the cross, antiphons, hymns and other appropriate compositions
are sung or recited. Some of these are of great

antiquity, and even in translation they impress us by their beauty and depth.

The first antiphon surprises us by its joyful character: "We worship you, Lord, we venerate your cross, we praise your resurrection. Through your cross you brought joy to the world." If the cross is never absent from the Christian life, neither is joy. Even on Good Friday we could meditate on the joy of Christ, the joy of total sacrifice.

Next come the famous *Improperia* or "Reproaches", so called because in these verses Christ reproaches his people for their ingratitude. He recounts all his favours on their behalf: he led them out of Egypt, brought them safely through the desert, fed them with manna, worked all sorts of wonders for them; in return for all these favours they treated him with contempt. Antithesis such as: "I led you out of Egypt from slavery to freedom, but you led your Saviour to the cross", is used to effect throughout the whole composition. Interspersed between the reproaches we have the poignant refrain: "My people, what have I done to you? How have I offended you? Answer me!", and then the *Trisagion*: "Holy is God! Holy and strong! Holy immortal One, have mercy on us!"

Christ reproaches all of us, not only those who crucify him. But he does so in a gentle way which arouses our compassion rather than feelings of guilt. It is our ingratitude and hardness of heart that are questioned. The only response to these questions and reproaches is the silent one of kissing the feet of the crucified Lord.

These *Improperia* combine religious sentiment

with theological perception. For the Christ, who
appeals to his people, is the pre-existent Word. As
Word of God, he was present and at work throughout all the stages of sacred history; he guided the
chosen people, he shaped the course of their
history. He is the Word Incarnate; and while the
memory of his sufferings elicits our compassion,
we may not for a moment forget that he is the All
Holy One.

The faithful continue to file up to the cross, and
now the choir begins the hymn *Pange lingua*. This
hymn[8] has been likened to a victory march. It recounts the glorious victory which Christ won over
his adversary Satan. Then in one strophe it evokes
the scene of the crucifixion in all its cruel reality;
but even here the redemptive value of these sufferings is not lost sight of. Then in a note of great
tenderness the poet addresses the cross itself, beg-
ging it to relax its rigour. Here we have a splendid
blending of ancient and medieval devotion to the
cross and passion.

## The glory of the cross

That great pontiff and father of the Church, Pope
St Leo, has left us in his sermons many beautiful
and arresting thoughts on the passion and cross of
the Lord, which may help our Good Friday meditations.[9]

In Sermon 55 he says that "Christ's passion contains the mystery of our salvation"; that it is for us
"the stepping-stone to glory" and that it symbolises
"the true altar of prophecy".

On Tuesday of the fifth week of Lent, in the
office of readings (*Divine Office* II, pp. 217-19),
we have one of his finest sermons on the passion.
In it he refers to "the glory of the cross which
shines on heaven and earth". Then there is that un-
forgettable passage:

> O wonderful power of the cross! O indescri-
> bable glory of the passion! There is the tribunal
> of the Lord, and the judgment of the world,
> and the power of the crucified one.

The cross is "the source of all blessings, the cause
of all graces".

In a sermon preached on Passion Sunday, he
could even speak of "the feast of the Lord's
passion" (*festivitas dominicae passionis*). This may
sound like a contradiction in terms but not if we
view the work of redemption as a unified whole, as
the fathers of the Church did. Viewed with the
eyes of faith, contemplated in the light of Christ's
Easter victory, the cross is indeed "the trophy of
his triumph" and "the adorable sign of salvation".
For that reason the joy of Easter does not obliterate
the memory of the passion and Calvary; in fact, in
the time of Pope St Leo the gospel reading for
Easter included the account of the passion together
with that of the resurrection of the Lord.[10]

## The communion rite

The altar is now covered with a cloth and the cor-
poral and book are placed on it. The ciborium,
containing the hosts consecrated at last evening's
Mass, is brought to the altar. Two ministers with

lighted candles accompany the priest or deacon,
and place their candles on or near the altar.

The usual Mass prayers of preparation for the
reception of the sacrament follow: the Lord's
Prayer with its embolism and acclamation and the
priest's private prayer of preparation; then the
showing of the Host with the words, "This is the
Lamb of God", and the response, "Lord, I am not
worthy".

What is the special significance of our communion
this day? In answer to this question we may cite St
Paul who alludes to a deep and mysterious relationship between sacramental communion and the passion and death of Christ. In his instructions on the
Lord's Supper he reminds the Corinthians: "Until
the Lord comes, therefore, every time you eat this
bread and drink this cup, you are proclaiming his
death" *(1 Cor 11:25-26).*

But the eucharist is not only a proclamation, it
is also a participation in the death of Christ. It is a
communion with the body and blood of Christ,
that is, with Christ in his state of sacrificial victim.
(See *1 Cor 10:15-16.)*

Christ is our sacrificial food. To receive his body
and blood is to enter into his disposition of total
self-offering to the Father; it is to be drawn into
the same movement of loving sacrifice. That is
what participation means at its deepest level, and it
is beautifully expressed by Pope St Leo in the following passage:

> For naught else is effected by the partaking of
> the Body and Blood of Christ than that we pass

into that which we take (*ut in id quod sumimus transeamus*), and both in spirit and in body carry everywhere him, in and with whom we were dead, buried and rose again.

Our Good Friday communion therefore proclaims and witnesses to the passion and death of the Lord; it enables us to participate at the deepest level in Christ's sacrifice and to associate ourselves with it; and finally it gives us a share in the fruits of that sacrifice.

When all have received communion, a period of silent prayer is observed; priest and people meditate on the sacrament they have received. We thank the Lord who, in this sacrament, has left us a wonderful memorial of his suffering and death, and also a pledge of future glory.

The service is concluded with the prayer after communion, followed by a prayer of blessing. The former refers to the healing and transforming power of the sacrament; it asks for a generous spirit of service in those who have taken part in the celebration. Among the blessings invoked on the assembly, that of stronger faith is especially important. Faith is the foundation of all the virtues.

The Good Friday liturgy is at an end. There is no dismissal or recessional hymn. People depart in silence. Some remain to continue their own prayers and devotions. Those who did not have an opportunity to kiss the cross may now do so. Others may make the stations of the cross.

The altar is stripped bare, the tabernacle is empty, the sanctuary devoid of flowers or other ornamentation. On no other day of the year are our churches so austere in appearance. Nothing distracts our attention from the altar and the crucifix. The Church keeps vigil by the cross of the Lord.

# 11 Holy Saturday

> On Holy Saturday the Church waits at the
> Lord's tomb, meditating on his suffering and
> death. The altar is left bare and the sacrifice of
> the Mass is not celebrated. Only after the solemn
> vigil during the night, held in anticipation of
> the resurrection, does the Easter celebration
> begin, with a spirit of joy that overflows into
> the following period of fifty days.

This introductory note from the missal explains
the character of the day. We are to refrain from
premature rejoicing as the Easter celebration has
not yet begun. It is a day of quiet waiting, or
prayerful preparation for the resurrection. There is
still sorrow, even if it lacks the intensity of the preceding day. The early Christians fasted as strictly
on this day as on the Friday, for this was the time
when Christ the Bridegroom was taken from them
*(Mt 2:19-21)*.

If we can spend this day in quiet and prayerful
waiting, our time will have been well spent. In the
beautiful homily, chosen for today's office of
readings, it is this mood which is evoked:

> Today there is a great silence on earth; a great
> silence and then solitude; a great silence because
> the King sleeps; the earth trembled and was

silent, because God has gone to sleep in the flesh, and has awakened those who have slept from of old.

On the first Holy Saturday all seemed lost. The disciples were scattered, a small dispirited band of men, their hopes shattered. Only Mary kept faith and awaited the resurrection of her Son. That is why on Saturdays throughout the year the Church commemorates the Virgin Mary, and there is a votive Mass and office in her honour.

A note of serenity, even of joyful expectancy, pervades the Holy Saturday liturgy. Christ has died, but his death is like a sleep from which he will awake on Easter morning.

The psalms chosen for the office of readings are redolent of quiet trust and expectancy. It is as though Christ himself were praying them. In Psalm 4 the verse "I will lie down in peace and sleep comes at once" is applied to Christ in the tomb confidently awaiting the resurrection. Again in Psalm 15 we have wonderful expressions of hope: "For you will not leave my soul among the dead, nor let your beloved know decay. You will show me the path of life, the fullness of joy in your presence, at your right hand happiness for ever."

The scripture reading *(Heb 4:1-13)* speaks to us of the sabbath day of rest prepared for God's people after the labours of this life. It concludes: "There must still be, therefore, a place of rest reserved for God's people, the seventh-day rest, since to reach the place of rest is to rest after your work, as God did after his."

In the ancient homily from which we have already quoted, a dialogue takes place between Christ and Adam. Christ enters the abode of the dead and awakens Adam, saying to him: "Arise from the dead; I am the life of the dead. Arise, O man, work of my hands, arise, you who were fashioned in my image. Rise, let us go hence; for you in me and I in you, together we are one undivided person."

We all share in the mystery of Holy Saturday. St Paul reminds us of this: "When we were baptised we went into the tomb with him and joined him in death, so that as Christ was raised from the dead by the Father's glory, we too might live a new life" *(Rm 6:4)*. In the ancient Church the symbolism of baptism as burial with Christ was more obvious than in later times. Baptism was by immersion; the adult catechumens really went down into the baptismal font which in appearance was not unlike a tomb. They descended into the waters as a sign of death and burial; they emerged from the font signifying the resurrection.

Our participation in the burial of Christ is evoked in the prayers which conclude the office. In the final petition of morning prayer we ask: "Christ, Son of the living God, you enabled us to be buried with you in baptism; grant that, being conformed to your resurrection, we may walk in newness of life." And in the concluding prayer we ask: "Grant that your faithful people, who were buried with him in baptism, may, by his resurrection, obtain eternal life."

# 12 The Easter Vigil

With the approach of nightfall we have arrived at the heart of our Holy Week celebrations. It is the hour of the great Vigil, the Easter Vigil, which St Augustine described as "the mother of all vigils".

For the Christians of antiquity Easter was not just one feast among many, it was rather "the feast of feasts". And it was essentially in the night vigil, culminating in the Mass of the resurrection, that they celebrated this feast.

The Church of our time has rediscovered the deep significance of Easter as the celebration of the paschal mystery. Thanks to the restored rites of Holy Week, begun under Pope Pius XII and completed since Vatican II, the pre-eminence of Easter in the liturgical year is secured. Holy Week constitutes the heart of the liturgical year and the Easter Vigil lies at the heart of Holy Week.

Why is the Easter Vigil so important? Why does the Church urge us to take part in this long-drawn-out liturgy, held at such an inconvenient hour? It is not just because it is ancient and traditional but because of its profound meaning and inner value. Here at the heart of Easter we are celebrating the mystery of human redemption. According to the definition of Odo Casel, Easter, the Christian pasch, is "the feast of human redemption through the death and resurrection of the Lord."[1]

In the course of the liturgical year the Church commemorates the various aspects of the work of redemption. On this occasion it celebrates it as a whole in all its amplitude. This is the paschal feast which includes all the other Christian mysteries. Because of our union with Christ through faith and baptism, we ourselves are intimately associated with the dying and rising of Christ. In celebrating the paschal mystery of Christ, the Church celebrates her own passing-over from death to life.

## The Jewish pasch

This most Christian of feasts has its roots in the Old Testament, and to understand it we must first consider the Jewish passover. Divine providence has linked the two celebrations, and even the name "pasch" is of Hebrew origin. (The Latin *pascha*, the French *pâque* and even the Irish *cásc* derive from the Hebrew word.)

The Jewish passover was celebrated on the fourteenth day of the spring month of Nisan. It commemorated the deliverance of the Israelites from their life of oppression and servitude in Egypt. It was a feast of redemption, of liberation. The blood of the lamb, sprinkled on the doorposts, underlined its redemptive character; for the destroying angel passed over the households preserved by the blood of the lamb.

In fact this feast contained the memory of all God's wonderful deeds in the course of history;

deliverance from the hand of the enemy, the giving of the covenant on Mount Sinai, the wonders of the exodus and final entry into the promised land. It also commemorated the "birth" of God's people. From being an oppressed minority in the land of Egypt, it became a people, a nation, God's "very own possession".

The passover was the great event in the history of Israel. Its commemoration in the yearly paschal festival was the great feast of the Jewish people. We read in chapter 12 of the book of Exodus:

> It is the night of the pasch, the Lord's passing by. . . . You are to observe this day as a memorial of the past, a day when you keep holiday in the Lord's honour. . . . It is a night for keeping vigil in the Lord's honour, this night when he led them out of the land of Egypt.

Its celebration was not merely a recalling of what had happened in the distant past, but a memorial through which the past event became a present reality and those who celebrated it felt themselves caught up and made sharers in the experience of their forefathers. To the present day, devout Jews celebrate the passover with a keen sense of personal participation, as is evident from the words of their ritual: "It was not our ancestors only, that the Most High (blessed be he) redeemed from Egypt, but us also did he redeem with them."

## The Christian pasch

It was not by chance that Christ endured his passion and underwent death on our behalf at the time of the Jewish pasch. It is part of a divine plan and of a divine pedagogy. In his sacrifice on the cross Christ is shown to be the fulfilment of the ancient passover. In the words of St Paul, "Christ, our passover, has been sacrificed" *(1 Cor 5:7)*.

Among the New Testament writers St John takes special care to show the correspondence between the events of the passover and the mysteries of Christ's life. He shows, for example, how Christ fulfils the major types of the exodus. He is the new Moses leading his people to freedom; he feeds them with the new manna which is the eucharist; he gives them to drink from the fountain of living water. He is the bronze serpent and all who look upon him with faith are saved. He is the light shining in the darkness, a more perfect light than that which led the Israelites through the desert. He is the true paschal lamb.[2]

St John begins his account of the Last Supper with the words which evoke the passover and its celebration: "It was before the festival of the passover, and Jesus knew that the hour had come for him to pass from this world to the Father" *(Jn 13:1)*. In this mysterious passage Christ achieves a more wonderful deliverance than that of Moses. In his passing through death from this world to the Father, Christ delivers all men from the servitude of sin.

The passion narrative of St John is full of Old Testament reminiscences, quite a few of which relate to the passover celebration. According to John, it is at the hour of the evening sacrifice, when the paschal lambs are being slain in the Temple, that Jesus is crucified. John also tells us that in fulfilment of what was said of the paschal lamb the soldiers did not break his legs: "Not a bone of his shall be broken." (See *Exodus 12:46.*)

Easter then is the true paschal feast, it celebrates the paschal mystery of Christ and his Church. It is a feast of redemption, and it is especially in the liturgy of the Easter Vigil that the Church celebrates that feast. In it we celebrate Christ's victory over sin and death, his opening up to mankind of a new life in God. Through our sharing in his death and resurrection, we ourselves gain access to the kingdom of light and freedom.

## The vigil service

The vigil is divided into four parts: a service of light; a liturgy of the word; a baptismal service; the paschal eucharist.

## Service of Light

The theme of light is a constant one in the Easter liturgy. It is appropriate that the vigil should begin with the blessing of the Easter fire and the lighting of the paschal candle.

Ideally, the service will begin outside the church, in front of the porch, where a large fire has been prepared. The people gather round the fire in a circle. Easter is a complete new beginning for the world. That is the symbolism of the new fire and the new light.

This fire ritual is pre-Christian, but because of its rich symbolism it has been assumed into the Church's liturgy. Here in Ireland, we may associate the Easter fire with that which St Patrick is said to have lit one Easter evening on the Hill of Slane before appearing in the presence of King Laoghaire at Tara .[3] However, if there are pagan vestiges in this ritual, they are at once dispelled by the opening words of the priest:

> Dear friends in Christ,
> on this most holy night,
> when our Lord Jesus Christ passed from death
>     to life,
> the Church invites her children
>     throughout the world
> to come together in vigil and prayer.
> This is the passover of the Lord. . . .

The new fire is blessed; from it the paschal candle will be lit. Attention now turns to this candle, an extra large and beautiful one, which throughout the whole Easter season, will serve as a symbol of Christ.

To fit it out for its symbolic role, the candle may be suitably marked, following medieval tradition. First the priest cuts a cross in the wax with a stylus. Then he traces the Greek letter *Alpha* above the cross and the letter *Omega* below. These are the first and last letters of the Greek alphabet. "I am the alpha and omega, the first and the last, the beginning and the end", says Christ in the Book of Revelation *(22:13)*.

Between the arms of the cross the numerals of the current year, e. g. 1976, are inscribed. Christ is thus shown to be the "King of all ages". For us Christians, every year is a year of the Lord, since we profess that all times and seasons belong to him. In the formula accompanying the incisions, the priest says:

Christ yesterday and today
the beginning and the end
Alpha and Omega
all times belong to him
and all ages
to him be glory and power
through every age and for ever. Amen.

The priest may now insert five grains of incense in the candle to represent the wounds the Saviour received on head, feet, hands and side. This he does in the form of a cross, saying: "By his holy and glorious wounds may Christ our Lord guard us and keep us."

The candle is lit from the new fire with the words: "May the light of Christ, rising in glory, dispel the darkness of our hearts and minds."

Then a procession forms. The priest or deacon takes the Easter candle, lifts it high and acclaims: "Christ our light", to which all respond: "Thanks be to God." Then all enter the darkened church, led by the candle-bearer.

At the church door the candle is lifted high a second time, again with the acclamation "Christ, our light" and the response "Thanks be to God." At this point all the members of the congregation have their small candles lit from the flame of the paschal candle. This conveys the idea that the light, which is Christ, must be communicated. This happens when the Gospel is preached, when men accept it with faith and are baptised. Faith is a gift of God, but, as the human instruments of God, we help to mediate that faith to others.

When the priest or deacon carrying the candle arrives before the altar, he turns round to face the people and makes his acclamation for the third and last time. The people take their places in the pews and the lights of the church are put on. The candle is placed on its stand in the sanctuary.

The Easter Song of Praise, also known as the *Exultet* now follows. As the Latin word suggests, it is a hymn of joy and exultation in praise of God, the author of light and the giver of life and salvation. It was the custom among the Jews to say a prayer of blessing at the time of lighting the evening lamp in the home. This custom was taken over into Christian usage, and the Church's evening prayer, known in early times as *lucernarium* (from *lucerna*, a lamp), developed out of it. The magnificent formula of praise and blessing said before the paschal candle is but an elaborate form of what was commonplace in Christian antiquity.

It begins with a three-fold invitation to rejoice: "Rejoice, heavenly powers, Rejoice, O earth, Rejoice, O Mother Church". It is, of course, the redemption of mankind, in all its phases and aspects, that is the cause of the Church's rejoicing.

The whole of salvation history is there in poetic form: the passover of the Hebrews, of Christ and of the Church. The great wax candle evokes at once the pillar of fire that led the Israelites across the desert and Christ the Light of the world; it is the light of revelation, of baptism and of final glory.

The *Exultet* is one of the literary and theological treasures of the Roman liturgy. In it praise, thanksgiving and supplication are blended in a splendid unity. Ideally it should be sung; the vernacular text has been set to music.[4] It is accorded the same honours as the proclamation of the gospel. All remain standing holding their lighted candles while it is being sung.

## The Liturgy of the Word

After the Easter Song of Praise the candles are put out and all sit down for the Liturgy of the Word. This consists of readings, canticles and prayers. The reading of the word of God is "the fundamental element of the Easter Vigil". There are nine readings altogether, culminating in the gospel of the Mass. For pastoral reasons the number of readings may be reduced, but it should be borne in mind that the Church attaches great importance to these readings.[5]

To relieve monotony it is preferable to have several readers. Good readers can make a scriptural text come alive. The Old Testament readings, in particular, lend themselves to a certain dramatic interpretation.

The whole atmosphere in which this service of readings is carried out should be relaxed and unhurried. We must dispose ourselves to listen attentively to the word of God. Here is set before us a whole synopsis of salvation history, God's great plan to redeem the world. In the books of the Old Testament that plan unfolds itself, in the New

Testament it finds realisation. It is the story of God's love for the world.

## First reading

The first reading is the account of creation *(Gen 1:1—2:2)*. There is great optimism in the Old Testament vision of creation and in the repeated refrain, "God saw that it was good." Creation mirrored the perfections of God himself.

But the God of creation is also the God of redemption. In admiring his handiwork in nature, the Church is drawn to contemplate his wonders in the order of grace. For this is a baptismal vigil: on this night the sacrament of re-birth is conferred or renewed. And even in this first reading Christian tradition finds a baptismal typology. The Spirit of God that "hovered over the water" in the beginning is the same Holy Spirit who sanctifies the waters of baptism. The creation of light on the first day also suggests baptism, the sacrament of enlightenment.

Baptism is a new creation. We read in *Genesis* how God created man in his own image. This image was disfigured by sin and needed to be restored by Christ's redeeming work. Through faith and baptism that redemption becomes operative in us. St Paul reminds the newly-baptised: "You have stripped off your old behaviour with your old self, and you have put on a new self which will progress towards true knowledge the more it is renewed in the image of its maker" *(Col 3:10)*. Elsewhere he says: "Therefore, if anyone is in Christ, he is a new creation; the old has passed away, behold, the new has come" *(2 Cor 5:17).*

In this liturgical reading of the Old Testament we are operating, so to speak, on two levels. The Church reads into this account of creation the mystery of re-creation, that is, of redemption. This is made explicit in the prayer which follows the reading and psalm:

> Almighty and eternal God,
> you created all things
>     in wonderful beauty and order.
> Help us now to perceive
> how still more wonderful is the new creation
> by which in the fullness of time
> you redeemed your people
> through the sacrifice of our passover,
>     Jesus Christ.

## Second reading

The restoration of this reading *(Gen 22:1-18)* to the Easter Vigil liturgy (from which it had been dropped in a previous reform) has been greatly appreciated. Christian tradition has always attached it closely to the paschal mystery, and in the Old Testament it was read in the context of the passover.[6]

Briefly, it recounts how Abraham, in obedience to a divine command, prepares to sacrifice his only and much-loved son, Isaac. At the last moment an angel appears and orders him not to raise his hand against the boy. It was his obedience that was being put to the test. Instead of his son, a ram is offered as a burnt sacrifice. In conclusion, Abraham is promised the reward of his obedience: he will become the father of many nations.

Abraham would not even spare his beloved child Isaac. We find echoes of this in the New Testament with reference to Christ. St John tells us: "Yes, God loved the world so much that he gave his only Son, so that everyone who believes in him may not be lost but have eternal life" *(Jn 3:16)*. This was a more perfect sacrifice since God spared Isaac but did not spare his own Son. However, God's mercy did not detract from Abraham's unconditional obedience which prefigured that of Christ himself, who was "obedient unto death". Isaac, too, is a "type" of Christ. Not only is he innocent, but willingly allows himself to be sacrificed. Christ offers no resistance to his captors; he is led like a sheep to slaughter.

If the sacrifice of Christ is foreshadowed here, so is his resurrection. The author of *Hebrews* alludes to this: "By faith Abraham, when he was tested, offered up Isaac. . . He considered that God was able to raise men even from the dead; hence he did receive him back, and this was a symbol" *(Heb 11: 17-20*; RSV version).

Finally, we may consider how fruitful was the obedience of Abraham: God would shower blessings upon him; his descendants would be as numerous as the stars of heaven and as the grains of sand on the seashore. How much more fruitful is the sacrifice of Christ by which the world is reconciled with God, and men and women are united as children of the one Father. It is through the sacrifice of Christ that the promises made to Abraham are fulfilled. (See concluding prayer.)

## Third reading

So important is this reading *(Ex 14:15—15:1)* for an understanding of the paschal mystery that it may not be omitted. It describes the miraculous crossing of the Red Sea by the Israelites. This was the great breakthrough to freedom of God's people, an event of decisive importance in their history.

Here redemption is presented as a victory. The crossing of the Red Sea was a disaster for Pharaoh and his army; for the Israelites it was a triumph and deliverance. It symbolised the victory of God over the powers of evil.

The redemption accomplished by Christ was also a victory; and it was as a victory that the early fathers of the Church liked to understand it. It was a battle fought between Christ and his adversary, Satan. Here goodness was pitted against evil, light against darkness: "Death with life contended: combat strangely ended! Life's own champion, slain, yet lives to reign" (Sequence for Easter Sunday). From this struggle, in which at first Satan seems to triumph, Christ emerges victorious.

Through baptism the Christian shares in the victory of Christ. The waters of baptism are a force for life and death: life for those who are cleansed by these waters, death to all that is opposed to the reign of God. Like the Israelites of old, the newly-baptised pass through the waters of the Red Sea: they leave behind them the world of darkness and slavery and with Christ (the new Moses) at their head, they set out for the promised land.

It will be noted that the responsorial psalm is

actually a continuation of the reading. Here the
narrative breaks into song: "I will sing to the Lord,
glorious his triumph!" It is the victory song of the
people of God, the canticle of Moses and the sons
of Israel. It is also the victory song of the people of
God of the New Testament; it is the thanksgiving
song of those whom Christ has redeemed. On Easter
night we sing it with exultation. St John heard it
sung in the New Jerusalem: "They all had harps
from God, and they were singing the hymn of Moses
the servant of God, and of the Lamb" *(Rev 15:3)*.

## The covenant theme

The next four readings, all from the Prophets, may
be grouped together under the theme of covenant.
They speak of God's redeeming love, of the everlasting covenant he has made with his people; they
exhort us to be faithful to that covenant, to give
our wholehearted allegiance to the Law of God.

The fourth reading *(Is 54:5-14)* expresses the
covenant relationship between God and his people.
It is no mere legal arrangement, but resembles
rather the marriage contract. It is a partnership of
love which demands mutual trust, generosity and
fidelity. Where these qualities are lacking, the
relationship is under strain. It can break down
completely if either party is unfaithful.

Time and again Israel has been unfaithful to the
marriage contract between God and his people, but
God never annulled that contract nor disowned the
unfaithful spouse. His love conquers. Where there
has been alienation there is now reconciliation.

How beautifully this is expressed in the lines:

> In excess of anger, for a moment
> I hid my face from you.
> But with everlasting love
> I have taken pity on you,
> says the Lord, your redeemer.

God reaffirms the marriage contract. He swears that his love will never depart from his people; his "covenant of peace" will never be shaken.

This reading draws attention to a fundamental aspect of the redemption, namely, the divine love which inspired it. Love, undeserved and unreciprocated, is the ultimate explanation and the motive-force of man's redemption. In celebrating the feast of human redemption at Easter we are brought face to face with the mystery of divine love.

Again in the fifth reading *(Is 55:1-11)* we meet the covenant idea, but now the accent is more on our response to the covenant than on the "divine pity".

"With you I will make an everlasting covenant", says the Lord. In the Old Testament the passover feast commemorated, among other marvels, the giving of the covenant. For the Church of the New Testament, Easter celebrates the establishment of the "new and eternal covenant" which was sealed in the blood of Christ. In Christ, the mediator of that covenant, all the promises made to the patriarchs and prophets are fulfilled.

As God's people, we must be faithful to the terms of the covenant. The giving must not be all on God's side. His love and fidelity must be

answered by our love and fidelity; otherwise there
is no real covenant relationship. Christ is our model:
as head of redeemed humanity he offered to the
Father the perfect response of obedience and love.

In the sixth reading *(Bar 3:9-15, 32—4:4)* the
prophet, as spokesman of God, makes an impas-
sioned appeal to Israel to be converted and to
return to the Lord. His words challenge us as they
challenged the Jewish nation in the time of the
Babylonian captivity.

Conversion must be expressed in a ready acceptance of the Law of God. This means that our lives
must correspond with that law and be in conformity
with it. That is another way of saying that we must
keep our part of the covenant.

For us Christians this means living according to
the gospel of Christ in which the Old Law finds its
fulfilment. It demands of us not only the acceptance of individual commandments but our willingness to live according to the spirit of the New Law.

The prophet Baruch presents us with a beautiful
and compelling vision of a life lived in accordance
with the Law. It is a life blessed with peace,
strength and happiness. The Law is not something
legalistic and narrowly conceived, but a whole way
of life. It is the embodiment and living expression
of wisdom.

The seventh and final Old Testament reading
*(Ezk 36:16-28)* contains God's promise to pardon
his unfaithful people, to gather them from among
the nations and restore them to their own land.
Redemption is here seen as a work of restoration
and reunification. Sin is the cause of division and

dispersal. Christ, redeemer of mankind, has effected a more perfect restoration: he has gathered people of all nations into the unity of his body; between Christ and his members no closer unity could be conceived.

Then there is a prophetic utterance which again sounds the theme of baptism: "I shall pour clean water over you and you will be cleansed." The Church fathers saw in this an allusion to the purifying waters of baptism. The responsorial psalm, with its refrain "Like the deer that longs for running streams. . .", expresses the longing of the catechumen for the sacrament of baptism.

The concluding part of the reading is taken up with the covenant theme. Henceforth God's law will be obeyed not just in a literal way but from the heart. This is made possible by the fact that God will transform the human heart, making it capable of generous response. A relationship which is even more intimate than that of natural kinship is thus established between God and man. This is the true covenant relationship, expressed in those words which appear as a kind of refrain in the Bible: "You shall be my people and I will be your God."

The prayer which follows the seventh reading may be considered as a summing up of the whole series of Old Testament readings. There is a choice of two prayers. The first expresses the plea that God may carry forward and bring to completion the work of redemption begun long ago; it is a prayer for renewal for the Church and mankind. The second formula asks for a deeper understanding of the love which motivated the passover mystery.

## Easter glory

It sometimes happens that, at the end of a long journey, we are rather taken by surprise that we have reached our destination. One may have a similar experience on Holy Saturday night. The transition from Old Testament prophecy to the full splendour of Easter is sudden and almost imperceptible. After the seventh reading, with its responsory and prayer, the altar candles are lighted for Mass. There is no break in the sequence, but a gentle transition from darkness to light. The waiting is over, Easter has now arrived.

The celebrant intones the *Gloria*, that joyful prose-hymn which we have inherited from Christian antiquity. It is recited or chanted at every festive Mass outside Lent. Traditionally it is closely associated with Easter, for, according to ancient Roman custom, it could be said or sung by ordinary priests only at the Mass of the vigil.[7] It expresses praise, adoration and humble supplication. To heighten the note of joy, the bells of the church may be rung, heralding far and wide the good news of the resurrection.

This is followed by the opening prayer of the Mass. The grace we ask for is that of the spirit of sonship and of renewal; thus renewed, we shall be enabled to offer God the whole-hearted service which is his due.

The first of the New Testament readings is taken from the letter of St Paul to the Romans *(6:3-11)*.

The apostle penetrates to the heart of the Easter mystery. He explains how, through the sacrament of baptism, we participate in the paschal mystery of Christ. Christ, our head, suffered, died, was buried and rose again. Through baptismal grace, we, the body, are made to share, in a real and most intimate way, in this mysterious passage from death to life.

Baptism is a new beginning. The old way of life is left behind. It confers on us the status of children of God. Henceforth we share in the life of the risen Christ. Christian moral conduct must now accord with the dignity of our calling. Our life must be lived in and with Christ for God our Father. This calls for a new attitude, a new orientation and sense of purpose. In this short reading a whole programme of Christian living opens out for us.

## The Easter Alleluia

After the reading all rise and the priest solemnly intones the *Alleluia* which is repeated by the congregation. This acclamation, so expressive of praise, joy and victory makes its return after the long period of Lent during which it was muted. No other acclamation is so characteristic of the Easter season than this single Hebrew word. Ideally it will be sung, and there is a beautiful plain chant melody to accompany it.

In his Easter homilies, St Augustine never tired of expounding the significance of the *Alleluia*, the cry which anticipates the liturgy of heaven. Here it heralds the gospel of the resurrection and Christ himself who is present and speaks to us in his word. That is the function of the *Alleluia* at every Mass, but it acquires its full significance on this night of Easter.

The *Alleluia*, thrice repeated, forms the people's refrain after each strophe of the responsorial psalm. The psalm chosen is the great Easter psalm, *Psalm 117*. Christian tradition has closely allied it to the Easter mystery, and for that reason we meet it constantly throughout the paschal season. As used in the liturgy of this time, it sings of the victory of the risen Christ, which is also the victory of those whom he has redeemed. Catechumens about to be received into the Church, sinners restored to grace, the whole people of God renewed by the discipline of Lent, all can make their own those words of the psalm which tradition applies to Christ in his resurrection: "The Lord's right hand has triumphed, his right hand raised me up. I shall not die, I shall live and recount his deeds."

## The gospel of the resurrection

The word gospel comes from an Old English word "godspel" which means good tidings. The gospel is indeed the good news of salvation, and the gospel of the resurrection which we hear on Easter night is the most joyful in the whole year.

The present lectionary provides that, in the course of the three-year cycle, we will hear in turn the resurrection narrative of Matthew, Mark and Luke. The gospel account according to John is read at the day-time Mass.

With good reason the Church has found a place for each gospel. Each sacred author describes what happened in his own way. The central message, however, is the same in each.

In Matthew's account, an angel tells the women: "I know you are looking for Jesus, who was crucified. He is not here, for he has risen, as he said he would." In the gospel of Mark a young man in a white robe declares to the three women: "You are looking for Jesus of Nazareth, who was crucified: he has risen, he is not here." Luke has two men in brilliant clothes who ask: "Why look among the dead for someone who is alive? He is not here, he is risen."

It is the fact of the resurrection, rather than the events surrounding it, which commands our faith. We believe and profess that Christ rose from the dead on Easter Sunday. That lies at the very heart of our Christian faith.

In the Easter liturgy the evangelists speak to us, and Christ speaks to us through them. The Church allows the gospels to speak for themselves without adornment or qualification. And the best disposition to hear and to benefit from the liturgical readings is to lay ourselves open to them with a simple faith and a readiness to obey their message.

The gospel of the resurrection (whether it is Matthew, Mark, Luke or John who is addressing us) is a message for here and now. It may be familiar to us all, but can we pretend to have fathomed the mystery to which it points? It challenges our faith, it invites serious thought about the very foundations of our Christian religion.

The resurrection is not only an event of history, it is an ever-present reality which affects the life of each one of us. It has changed the course of history and it can transform our lives.

## The baptismal liturgy

The celebration of the paschal mystery at Easter provides the most appropriate setting for the conferring of baptism. From as early as the second century the baptism of adult catechumens was linked with Easter; and even after the disappearance of the adult catechumenate in the sixth century, it continued to be the practice of the Roman Church for many centuries to baptise infants at Easter or at Pentecost.[8] In our own time this ancient practice has been revived; and it is not such a rare thing to have an adult or child baptised in the course of the Easter Vigil.

If there are candidates for baptism, the priest now invites the assembly to pray for them. At the moment of their reception into full membership of the Christian community, earnest intercession is made on their behalf; and as on similar occasions (ordinations, religious professions) when the candidates are about to embark on a new state of life, the litany of the saints is said or sung to invoke God's abundant blessing on them.

In this litany the Church on earth associates her prayer with that of the Church in heaven. Christ, his angels and saints are invoked on behalf of these "chosen ones" who now approach the waters of re-birth. The litany is representative of the great saints of every age, including our own. There is a special petition for those about to be baptised: "Give new life to these chosen ones by the grace of baptism."

The water itself must now be prepared by a solemn prayer of blessing. In this beautiful formula, which dates from the sixth century or earlier, there is set before us a biblical reflection on the mystery of baptism. The themes we met in the readings, e.g. the water that covered the earth in the beginning, the crossing of the Red Sea, recur here. They are completed by New Testament additions such as the baptism of Christ in the Jordan, the blood and water that flowed from his side on the cross.

The Holy Spirit, who hovered over the waters at the dawn of creation, who in the form of a dove descended on Jesus in the Jordan, is now invoked to sanctify the baptismal font. Water is the material agent by which, through the power of the Holy Spirit, man is purified from sin and vice and engendered to a new life. The baptismal font is the tomb in which we are buried to sin; it is also the maternal womb from which we are reborn as children of God.

The role of the Holy Spirit in sanctifying the water is forcefully evoked by the rite of plunging the paschal candle three times into the font, with the invocation: "We ask you, Father, with your Son to send the Holy Spirit upon the waters of this font." It is held in the water until the completion of the blessing.

The moment for baptism has now arrived. It is to be hoped that there will be some candidate or candidates, whether infant or adult. To be baptised on this particular night is to participate in a very special way in the celebration of the paschal mystery; the passage from death to life, symbolised and effected by baptism, coincides with the liturgical celebration of that mystery.

We are all now given the opportunity to renew and consolidate our baptismal commitment. This is one of the summits of the Easter celebration, one prepared for throughout the whole period of Lent.

All present stand with lighted candles and, at the invitation of the priest, renew their baptismal profession of faith. They first renounce Satan, his works and empty promises. They then profess their faith in the articles of the Creed.

This rite of renewal somehow knits the community together. All of us, whether priests, religious or lay persons, are united in the profession of one faith; we form one people of God; we are all God's faithful, that is, a people established in the profession of their baptismal faith.

It was all so easy at our own baptism. The sponsors made that profession for us. But to make that faith our own and to live by it in adult life is not easy. Our faith may have to withstand difficulties of all kinds, but we are given the grace to say and to mean "I do believe." The grace of Easter is the grace of a faith newly found. We not only profess that faith but also pledge ourselves to live by it, which means rejecting all that is contrary to our life in Christ.

Having concluded with a prayer, the priest sprinkles the people with the blessed water, thus reminding them again of their own baptism. During the rite of sprinkling some suitable baptismal chant may be sung.

## The eucharistic liturgy

The eucharistic liturgy begins in the usual way with the presentation of the gifts. A rubric recommends that the bread and wine be brought to the altar by the newly-baptised who are specially honoured since this is the Mass of their first communion.

The eucharist completes the divine work begun in us at baptism. Together with the sacrament of confirmation it completes the process of Christian initiation. It only remains for us to cooperate with divine grace in bringing this process to full maturity. We must by our moral conduct, aligned to the gospel and sustained by the sacraments, "become what we are", that is, grow into the full realisation of our status as adopted sons and daughters of God. This idea of completion is evoked in the prayer over the gifts: "May this Easter mystery of our redemption bring to perfection the saving mystery you have begun in us."

The particular significance of our Easter Mass and communion is the theme of the first preface:

> We praise you with greater joy than ever
> on this Easter night
> when Christ became our paschal sacrifice.
> He is the true Lamb who took away
>     the sins of the world.
> By dying he destroyed our death;
> by rising he restored our life.

This paschal note is again sounded in the Old Roman canon (Eucharistic Prayer I) which has appropriate insertions for the feast. The prayer known as the *Communicantes* begins: "In union with the whole Church we celebrate that day (night) when Jesus Christ, our Lord, rose from the dead in his human body."

The newly-baptised are singled out for mention: "Father, accept this offering from your whole family and from those born into the new life of water and the Holy Spirit with all their sins forgiven." This text draws attention to the powers conferred on us through baptism. This sacrament imparts to all its recipients a share in the priesthood of Christ and this enables them to participate in the offering of the eucharistic sacrifice.[9]

Active participation in the eucharist has its most perfect expression in sacramental communion. Through our sharing in the body and blood of Christ we are brought into the closest union with the sacrifice of our High Priest. This realisation finds joyful expression in the communion antiphon: "Christ has become our paschal sacrifice; let us feast with the unleavened bread of sincerity and truth, alleluia."

In the prayer after communion the grace asked for is that of unity:

Lord, you have nourished us
    with your Easter sacraments.
Fill us with the Spirit of your love
and make us all one in heart.

This is the intention for which Christ prayed at the

Last Supper: "that they may be one" *(Jn 17:11).*
This was the object of his sacrificial death, "to gather
into one the children of God who are scattered
abroad", and to draw all things to himself *(Jn 11:52;
12:32).* This unity is perfected by the Holy Spirit
who unites all the followers of Christ and forms
them into his Body the Church. It is in receiving
the body and blood of Christ that we are filled
with his Holy Spirit and become one body and one
spirit with him. (See Eucharistic Prayer III.)

Our Easter communion has made us more effective instruments of God's peace and love. Our mission is to spread the good news of his divine love
and to work for the fulfilment of God's loving
purpose in the world. It is to this task that we are
sent forth by the words of the priest: "Go in peace
to love and serve the Lord, alleluia, alleluia."

## Commemoration of our Lady

According to an ancient belief, Jesus, after his
resurrection, first appeared to his mother Mary.
This appearance is not recorded in the gospels; yet
it would indeed have been very fitting.[10] Whether
we accept it or not, it has given rise to a beautiful
custom preserved in some monastic communities.

At the conclusion of the Mass of the Easter Vigil,
the celebrant, ministers and community file out in
solemn procession from the sanctuary. At a specially
prepared place in the church, a picture or sculpture
of Our Lady of Sorrows has been set in position
surrounded by flowers. Here the procession halts. ·
The monks turn to face the *pietà*. A chanter intones

the *Regina Coeli* and this is taken up by the whole community. As Christ is supposed to have conveyed the joyful tidings of his resurrection first to his mother on Easter morning, so the Church now relives that scene in the words of the anthem:

> Joy fill your heart, O Queen most high, alleluia!
> Your Son who in the tomb did lie, alleluia!
> Has risen as he did prophesy, alleluia!

# 13 Easter Sunday

## Sunday morning

The traditional greeting of Russian and other Eastern-rite Christians when they meet at Easter, is: "The Lord has risen", to which the reply is "He has truly risen." This is certainly a more expressive exchange of greeting than the banal "Happy Easter!" It is only in the liturgy that we find appropriate expressions of the joy of Easter. The refrain for the invitatory psalm at the morning office corresponds to the Russian greeting: "The Lord has truly risen, alleluia."

In the course of time customs of various kinds have grown round the great religious festivals, in particular Christmas and Easter. One such custom in Irish tradition deserves attention.[1] It was the practice, especially in rural areas, for people to get up early on this Sunday morning to see the sun "dancing". It seems to me that this idea and the customs attached to it can be given a Christian interpretation, namely, that the whole of creation has a share in the joy of the resurrection. This is borne out by St Paul: "Creation still retains the hope of being freed, like us, from its slavery to decadence to enjoy the same freedom and glory as

119

the children of God" *(Rm 8:19-23)*. The redemption, won by Christ, extends to the whole universe.

## The Mass

The Church assembles a second time, now in the
full light of day, to celebrate the Easter eucharist.
The Easter candle, prominent on its high stand, is
lighted. The sanctuary is adorned with flowers.
White vestments symbolise joy, and it is with an
expression of rejoicing that the entrance antiphon
begins: "I have risen: I am with you once more;
you have placed your hand on me to keep me safe.
How great is the depth of your wisdom!" How
skilfully the Church employs the psalms to express
both the sorrows and the joy of Christ. Here it is
Christ who speaks, addressing the Father. He is
now risen, has now returned to the Father. This is
the cry of victory of the *whole* Christ, head and
members. In the words of one of the Easter Vigil
prayers, the fallen are lifted up, the old are made
new and all things brought to perfection.[2]

The opening prayer of the Mass asks for a
renewal in our moral lives corresponding to the
mystery of the resurrection: "Let our celebration
today raise us up and renew our lives by the Spirit
that is within us." The alternative prayer expresses
the same idea in a different form: "May the risen
Lord breathe on our minds and open our eyes that
we may know him in the breaking of bread, and
follow him in his risen life."

In the first reading, from the *Acts of the Apostles
(10:34, 37-43)*, it is St Peter who addresses us. He

bears witness to the resurrection of Jesus. In fact his discourse gives a résumé of the public life of our Lord, beginning with his baptism by John; every event of that life is shown to have saving power. The culmination of that life is the death and resurrection of the Lord.

The reality of the resurrection is strongly affirmed. Not only by the statement, "three days afterwards God raised him to life", but also by the assertion that after the resurrection the apostles had "eaten and drunk" with him. St Peter, the chief apostle, testifies to all this. He speaks as an eye-witness, but he also speaks from the experience of his personal faith enlightened by the Holy Spirit. This apostolic witness is important for our own acceptance of the faith. This discourse of Peter is not only a recounting of what happened in the life of Christ, it is a profession of faith, a proclamation of Christian belief.

This reading also contains the message that the salvation, won by Christ, is universal in scope: "All who believe in Jesus will have their sins forgiven through his name." Through faith all men have access to the saving power of his death and resurrection.

In the second reading St Paul, addressing the Colossian Christians (Col 3:1-4), exhorts them to live in accordance with their newly-acquired state. The resurrection of our bodies and the glory which is to be ours remains an object of hope; but through our intimate union with Christ we already enjoy a foretaste of our inheritance.

While still pilgrims on this earth we must constantly seek the Lord, for he is our life: "Let your thoughts be on heavenly things, not on the things that are on earth." However, St Paul is not urging us to neglect our human tasks nor the people with whom we live. That would be a false spirituality. We must be fully involved in the life of this world without being immersed in it or captivated by it. We must realise that our ultimate goal, our final destiny, is not here in this material world, but "hidden away with Christ in God", and that we await his coming and manifestation in order that our own true lives may be revealed.

The lectionary provides an alternative reading from the first letter of St Paul to the Corinthians *(5:7-8)*, in which he exhorts them to live lives of "sincerity and truth" since Christ our passover has been sacrificed.

The sequence, *Victimae paschali*, is a medieval composition which, in dramatic form, sums up the mystery of redemption. Sung to the plain chant melody, it conveys something of the excitement of the first Easter Sunday. It has the form of a hurried dialogue between ourselves and Mary Magdalene. Mary bears witness to what she has seen; and we, believers and disciples, also bear witness: "That Christ is truly risen from the dead we know." (We may note how the theme of victorious combat, so dear to the early Church fathers, recurs in the sequence.)

The gospel is that of St John *(20:1-9)*. Again we meet Mary Magdalene, arriving at the tomb "very early on the first day of the week" and discovering that it is empty. Her first reaction is one of consternation. She hurries off to tell the two disciples who, on hearing her report, vie with each other in racing to the tomb. John arrives first but allows Peter to enter the tomb first.

"Then the other disciple who had reached the tomb first also went in; he saw and he believed." This seeing and believing constitutes the climax of the gospel. The proclamation of the Easter gospel is intended to arouse in each liturgical gathering the same response of faith. This faith rests on the testimony of the apostles and on the inspired scriptures which reveal the plan of God.[3]

Today's celebration should make us more conscious of the paschal character of every Mass. The acclamations, with which we are so familiar, acquire a new depth of meaning at Easter-time. Thus, the acclamation, "Christ has died, Christ is risen, Christ will come again", seems most appropriate on this day. It echoes the Easter preface: "By dying he destroyed our death; by rising he restored our life." In the same preface Christ is designated as "the true Lamb who took away the sins of the world", which anticipates what the priest announces before communion: "This is the Lamb of God who takes away the sins of the world."

Our participation in the sacrifice and sacrament of the Mass enables us to live out more truly and more effectively the mystery begun in us at baptism. In the words of J. M. Tillard: "By his change of heart and repentance he (the Christian) enters into the death of Jesus; by the new quality of his acts and life he enters into the resurrection. Such is the paschal law of the Christian mystery."[4]

Finally, there is the eschatological note, highlighted in the liturgy of Easter, but never absent from the Church's celebration of the eucharist: every time we eat this bread and drink this cup we proclaim the death of the Lord until he comes *(1 Cor 11:26)*. At the prayer following the consecration (the *anamnesis*) we commemorate not only past mysteries but look forward to the Lord's coming in glory. Today's liturgy impresses on our minds what we already know, that the eucharist is the pledge of eternal life, the pledge of our own future resurrection. The sacred banquet of the eucharist is a foretaste of the eternal paschal feast: "Happy are those who are called to his supper!", that is, "to the wedding feast of the Lamb" *(Rev 19:9)*.

It is on this note of joyful expectation that the prayer after communion sums up our hopes and petitions: "Father of love, watch over your Church, and bring us to the glory of the resurrection promised by this Easter sacrament."

The solemn blessing, which may be used in the Easter season, also directs our thoughts to future glory: "May he fulfil his promises and bless you with eternal life. . . May you come to the feast which lasts forever."

## Sunday evening

The evening of Easter Sunday has many associations for us. It recalls for us, in the first place, the appearance of the Lord to the two disciples on the road to Emmaus, recorded in the gospel of St Luke

*(24:13-35)*. These two men walk along despon-
dently; they do not recognise the stranger who
joins them on the road. Together they discuss all
that had happened in those last days. Jesus rebukes
them for their lack of faith, and then explains to
them how everything foretold in the scriptures had
come about. Arriving at the inn, they invite their
companion to join them for a meal and to remain
with them for the night. And then, in the course of
the meal, their eyes are opened and they "recognised him at the breaking of bread".

If there is an evening Mass on Easter Sunday the
gospel reading may be that of St Luke, as described
above.[5] It is appropriate that this passage should
be read this Sunday evening; even if it does not
figure in the liturgy, we should not omit it in our
own reading of the scriptures.

"Stay with us, Lord, for evening is approaching
and the day is almost over." The Church makes
this pressing invitation her own. It is an appeal to
the Lord to abide with his people, to protect his
community. It is a cry which is heard frequently in
the liturgy of paschaltide.[6] It arouses in us those
sentiments so movingly expressed in the poem of
H. F. Lyte, "Abide with me; fast falls the eventide"
(See appendix to the Divine Office, no. 112).[7]

With second Vespers of Easter Sunday, the
paschal triduum is brought to a close. This evening
office of praise, thanksgiving and petition provides
a prayerful finale to the day's celebrations. In the
psalms, the canticle from The Book of Revelation
and the Magnificat, the Church expresses her
thanksgiving for redemption.

Christian tradition associates the newly-baptised with this evening office. The ceremony included a procession to the baptistry where, the evening before, these new Christians received the waters of re-birth. There they sang some psalms and the Magnificat as a grateful commemoration of the sacrament they had received. They also visited the chapel where they had been confirmed. This special Easter Vespers originated in Rome in the fifth or sixth century; from there it spread to other parts of Europe and has survived here and there down to our own times. It appealed so much to popular devotion that it was known as "the glorious office" (*officium gloriosum*).[8]

It was on this same evening, the first day of the week, that Jesus appeared to his disciples gathered together in the upper room in Jerusalem. The gospel recording this event is that of St John *(20: 19-31)*. It is read at Mass on the second Sunday of Easter, but on Easter Sunday the wonderful event which it recounts is commemorated in the Church's evening prayer. The Magnificat antiphon says: "On the evening of that Sunday, when the disciples were gathered behind locked doors, Jesus came and stood among them. He said to them, 'Peace be with you, alleluia'."

It is on this note of peace that Easter Sunday draws to an end. The celebration is not over, however: in an atmosphere of quiet and recollection it is continued at a more personal level. Together with the public and liturgical celebration there is "the intimate feast" of the heart.

Peace is Christ's special bequest to his disciples

and to us on this day. Through his paschal mystery he has restored peace between God and man. He is himself our peace. And with this peace goes a great joy. With the disciples we can exclaim: "We have seen the Lord and are glad."

# Notes

## 2   Lent and penance

1. Sermon 50, quoted by G. HUDON in *La Perfection Chrétienne d'après les Sermons de Saint Léon*, Editions du Cerf, Paris, 1959, p. 215.
2. In the early Church, before the institution of Lent, a rigorous fast was observed only on the two days before Easter, i. e. Good Friday and Holy Saturday. This fast was regarded as an intrinsic part of the Easter celebration itself. In the Liturgy Constituion of Vatican II (art. 110), an attempt was made to return to this ancient conception of the paschal fast: "But the paschal fast must be kept sacred. Let it be celebrated everywhere on Good Friday, and where possible be *prolonged throughout Holy Saturday* so that the joys of the Sunday may be attained with uplifted and clear mind."
3. In the early centuries public celebration of Mass was normally reserved to Sundays and greater feasts. This tradition was maintained in Rome for a long time. An exception was made, however, for the season of Lent. Between the sixth and eighth centuries in Rome the practice of daily Mass celebrated by the pope or his delegate became established. This included a solemn procession and full participation by the people of Rome. Thus daily celebration of the eucharist, with the faithful taking part and communicating, was one of the most characteristic features of the Roman Lent.
4. For text and commentary, see J. D. CRICHTON and G. WEBB, *The Ministry of Reconciliation:* A Commentary on the Order of Penance, G. Chapman, London, 1974.
5. Signs of a revival of penance, both public and private,

128

are reported from the USA. One can even speak of an "up-swing in confessions" there. See *Notitiae* 103, 1975, p.82.

# 3    Lent as preparation for baptism

1. *Ordo Initiationis Christianae Adultorum*. An interim English translation of this Ordo has been made by ICEL. See commentary by A. KAVANAGH, OSB, "The Norm of Baptism: The New Rite of Christian Initiation of Adults" in *Worship* 48, March 1974, pp. 143- 52.
2. See commentary of I. de la POTTERIE, "Jésus et les Samaritains" in *Assemblées du Seigneur* 16, Editions du Cerf, Paris, 1969, pp. 34-49.
3. Homily 44 on the gospel of St John.
4. See commentary of M. MORLET, "Le Dernier Signe de la Glorification de Jésus" in *Assemblées du Seigneur* 18, Editions du Cerf, Paris, 1971, pp. 11-25.

# 5    Introducing Holy Week

1. *"Majoris Hebdomadae."* Egeria begins her account of Holy Week in Jerusalem with the words: "The next day, Sunday, is the beginning of the Easter week or, as they call it here, *'The Great Week'.*" *Egeria's Travels*, 30, 1.
2. *The Great Week*: An explanation of the liturgy of Holy Week, Longmans, Green, London, 1958.
3. See J. A. JUNGMANN, SJ, "The History of Holy Week as the Heart of the Liturgical Year" in *Studies in Pastoral Liturgy*, ed. Placid Murray, OSB, The Furrow Trust, Maynooth, 1961, pp. 11-24.
4. An excellent English translation with full commentary is now available: *Egeria's Travels*, (ed. JOHN WILKINSON), SPCK, London, 1971.

# 6    Passion or Palm Sunday

1. The procession had its origin in Jerusalem (4th century) where it took place on Sunday evening. The people

assembled on The Mount of Olives and from there went
in procession into the city. They carried olive branches
and were accompanied by the bishop who represented
Christ. See *Egeria's Travels,* (ed. John Wilkinson),
pp. 132-33.
2. The procession was introduced to the Roman liturgy at
a comparatively late date, a fact which helps explain the
remarkable contrast between the processional texts and
those of the Mass. For history of Palm Sunday see. N.
MAURICE-DENIS, "Le dimanche des Rameaux" in *La
Maison-Dieu* 41, 1955, pp. 16-33; and A. CHAVASSE in
*L'Eglise en Prière*, (ed. A. G. MARTIMORT), Desclée,
Tournai, 1965, pp. 730-32.

## 8   The Easter triduum

1. Letter 36, published in *Saint Ambrose—Letters*, trans.
M. M. BEYENKA in *The Fathers of the Church* series,
Catholic University of America, Washington, 1967, p. 194.
2. "Sacratissimum triduum crucifixi, sepulti, resuscitati."
English translation of this letter to Januarius (Letter 55),
in vol. 12, *The Fathers of the Church* series. The passage
quoted occurs on p. 279.
3. *General Roman Calendar,* chapter 1, no. 28.

## 9   Holy Thursday

1. *The Divine Office* III, p. 274*, for the feast of St Januarius, office of readings.
2. *Constitution on the Sacred Liturgy* of the Second Vatican
Council, II, no. 47, trans. J. ROGERS in *Liturgy—
Renewal and Adaptation*, (ed. A Flannery, OP), Scepter,
Dublin, 1968.
3. *Egeria's Travels,* (ed. JOHN WILKINSON), SPCK, 1971,
pp. 134-35; see commentary pp. 74-75.
4. See N. LAZURE, "Le lavement des pieds" in *Jeudi Saint*
vol. 20, series *Assemblées du Seigneur*, Cerf, Paris 1973,
pp. 53-64.

5. Encyclical *Mysterium Fidei,* no. 63.

# 10  Good Friday

1. *Egeria's Travels,* (ed. JOHN WILKINSON), SPCK, 1971, p.138.
2. See *New Liturgy* 4, Winter 1974-75, p.20.
3. See H. CAZELLES, "La destinee du  Serviteur" in *Le Triduum Pascal,* vol. 21, series *Assemblées du Seigneur,* Cerf, Paris, 1969, pp. 7-15. Also W. HARRINGTON in *Scripture in Church* 14, pp. 211-12.
4. See C. BOURGIN, "La Passion du Christ et la nôtre" in *Le Triduum Pascal,* vol. 21 of *Assemblées du Seigneur,* pp. 16-21. Also W. HARRINGTON in *Scripture in Church,* 14, pp. 219-20.
5. Here I follow commentary of I. de la POTTERIE, "La Passion selon St Jean" in *Le Triduum Pascal,* vol. 21 of *Assemblées du Seigneur,* pp. 22-38.
6. In the fifth century they were part of the daily formula of the Mass. For history see *The Church at Prayer: The Eucharist,* (ed. A. G. MARTIMORT), Irish University Press, 1973, pp. 109-112.
7. *Egeria's Travels,* (ed. JOHN WILKINSON), SPCK, 1971, p. 137. The kissing of the cross is witnessed to in Rome from the seventh century.
8. Composed by Venantius Fortunatus (AD 530-600) on the occasion of the sending of a relic of the true cross to Queen Radegunde for the convent at Poitiers. See J. CONNELLY, *Hymns of the Roman Liturgy* Longmans, Green and Co., London, 1954, pp. 81-84.
9. Translation of his letters and sermons in vol. XII of the series *Nicene and Post-Nicene Fathers,* Parker and Co., Oxford and New York, 1895.
10. Sermon 72, *Nicene and Post-Nicene Fathers,* vol.12,p.184. Pope St Leo here says: "The text of the divinely inspired story has clearly shown the treachery of the Lord Jesus Christ's betrayal, the judgment by which he was condemned, the barbarity of his crucifixion, and the glory of his resurrection."
11. Sermon 63 on the Passion, in vol XII of *Nicene and Post-Nicene Fathers,* p. 177.

## 12  The Easter Vigil

1. DOM ODO CASEL, *La Fête de Pâques dans l'Eglise des Pères*, vol 37, series *Lex Orandi*, Cerf, Paris, 1963, p. 93. This is a translation from the German.
2. See *John 6:31-32; 7:37-39; 3:13-15; 8:12-13; 19:33-37*.
3. See J. WALTON TYRER, *Historical Survey of Holy Week*, Alcuin Club Collections, No. XXIX, Oxford University Press, 1932, pp. 148-49.
4. *The Exultet*, English text set to music by a monk of Glenstal, Liturgical Publications, Glenstal Abbey, Ireland.
5. "At least three readings from the Old Testament should be read, although for more serious reasons the number may be reduced to two. The reading of *Exodus 14*, however, is never to be omitted."
6. See J. BERNARD, "L'institution eucharistique" in *Jeudi Saint*, vol 20 of *Assemblées du Seigneur*, pp. 48-49.
7. See *The Church at Prayer: The Eucharist*, (ed. A. G. MARTIMORT), Irish University Press, 1973, p. 88.
8. See J. A. JUNGMANN, "The History of Holy Week" in *Studies in Pastoral Liturgy*, vol 1, (ed. Placid Murray, OSB), The Furrow Trust, Maynooth, 1961, p. 13. Also *L'Eglise en Prière*, (ed. A. G. MARTIMORT), Desclée, Tournai, 1965, p. 541.
9. See *General Instruction on the Roman Missal*, chapter 3, no. 62. CTS edition, London, 1973.
10. Cardinal Newman, among others, held this belief. The poet Rainer Maria Rilke wrote a beautiful poem entitled "The Consolation of Mary with the Risen Christ" which is inspired by this tradition. See *The Penguin Book of Lieder*, (ed. S. PRAWER), pp. 176-77.

## 13  Easter Sunday

1. For this and other customs see K. DANAHER, *The Year in Ireland*, The Mercier Press, Cork, 1972.
2. The prayer following the seventh reading.
3. D. MOLLAT, "La découverte du tombeau vide" in *Assemblées du Seigneur*, vol. 21, p. 100.

4. *Assemblées du Seigneur* 21, p. 110.

5. This gospel is also read on the third Sunday of Easter, Year A.

6. For example, versicle and response for prayer during the day (afternoon); Magnificat antiphon for evening prayer 1 of Sunday, week 3.

7. Throughout the year we have the prayer of vespers for Monday of the fourth week: "Stay with us, Lord Jesus, as evening falls; be our companion on our way. In your mercy inflame our hearts and raise our hope, so that, in union with our brethren, we may recognise you in the scriptures and in the breaking of bread."

8. J. GAILLARD, *Holy Week and Easter*, The Liturgical Press, Collegeville, 1957, pp. 159-60.

# Bibliography

## Historical background to Lent and Holy Week

JUNGMANN, J., *Public Worship*, Burns & Oates, London, 1965, pp. 180-201.

EISENHOFER, L. and LECHNER, J., *The Liturgy of the Roman Rite*, Herder (Freiburg), Nelson (Edinburgh-London) 1961, pp. 118-214.

MARTIMORT, A. (ed.), *L'Eglise en Prière*, Desclée, Tournai, 1965, pp. 711-732.

WILKINSON, J., (trans. and ed.), *Egeria's Travels*, SPCK, London, pp. 132-140. With commentary.

## Scriptural commentary

*Scripture in Church*, a periodical, published by Dominican Publications, Dublin. See Nos 1, 6 and 10 of this series which treat of the Sunday and weekday readings for Lent and Eastertide.

*Assemblées du Seigneur*, a series of short volumes on the readings for the liturgical year, published by Editions du Cerf, Paris. They are very complete and fully up-to-date. Vols.14-18 treat of Lent; vols.19-21 treat of Holy Week.

MAERTENS, T. and FRISQUE, J., *Guide for the Christian Assembly*, published by Biblica, Bruges, 1965, in five volumes. See vols.2 and 3; although now dated, can still be consulted with profit.

## Liturgical commentary

BOUYER, L., *The Paschal Mystery*, Allen & Unwin, London, 1951; a pioneer work which can still serve as background reading.

134

*A New Catechism*, New Authorised Edition with Supplement, Herder (New York), Search Press (London), 1970. See pp. 155-193, "The Way to Easter".

HOWELL, C., *Preparing for Easter* (Revised edition), Chapman, London, 1972.

LOHR, A., *The Mass through the year*, Vol. 1, Longmans (London), Newman Press (Westminster MD), 1958, pp. 118-312. Also *The Great Week*, same publishers and date. (Both works require revision.)

MURRAY, P. (ed.), *Studies in Pastoral Liturgy*, Vol.1, The Furrow Trust, Maynooth, 1961, pp. 11-24, 140-151.

*La Maison-Dieu*, periodical, published by Editions du Cerf, Paris, for French National Centre of Pastoral Liturgy. See, in particular, the following issues: Nos 56, 90 ("Penance"), 75 ("The Holy Cross"), 41, 45, 49, 67, 68 ("Holy Week").

## Theology of Easter

CASEL, O., *La Fête de Pâques dans l'Eglise des Pères*, Editions du Cerf, Paris, 1963. French translation of the great German work.

CHEVROT, G., *On the Third Day*—The Resurrection in the Gospel and in the Liturgy, Scepter, Dublin, 1961. The approach is spiritual and pastoral.

DURWELL, F., *The Resurrection*, Sheed & Ward, London. Recently republished in New Ark Library editions. A translation from the original *La Résurrection de Jésus, Mystère du Salut*. A fine theological synthesis.

O'COLLINS, G., *The Easter Jesus*, Darton, Longman and Todd, London, 1973.

WANSBROUGH, H., *The Resurrection*, St Paul Publications, Slough, England. A careful investigation of the scriptural evidence.